THE CENTERS OF CIVILIZATION SERIES

Thebes

IN THE TIME OF
AMUNHOTEP III

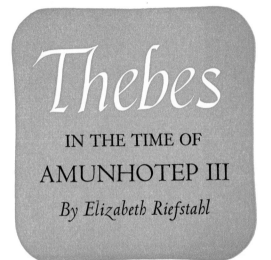

Thebes

IN THE TIME OF
AMUNHOTEP III
By Elizabeth Riefstahl

Norman

UNIVERSITY OF OKLAHOMA PRESS

Library of Congress Catalog Card Number: 64–11326

Copyright 1964 by the University of Oklahoma Press, Publishing Division of the University. Composed and printed at Norman, Oklahoma, U.S.A., by the University of Oklahoma Press. First edition.

To Claudia

WHO HAS RESENTED EVERY MOMENT

I HAVE DEVOTED TO

THE COMPOSITION OF THIS BOOK

Preface

WHEN I EMBARKED on this study of Thebes in its prime, I thought I could stick to facts. I had not gone far before I had to call imagination to my assistance. In this, I find myself in illustrious company. Few historians have been able to resist offering their own interpretations of the all-too-meager records of a long-vanished city and the civilization from which it sprang, and such interpretations show a wide variance of opinion. If the scope of this little book permitted footnotes, I could cite reputable authority for—and against!—most of the statements it contains. As it is, I can only apologize for the unexplained perhaps's and maybe's that lard its pages.

The bibliography I submit includes a mere handful of the books and articles I have consulted. I have selected from a vast literature only those titles which, it seemed to me, would be most helpful to students who wish to go more deeply into the civilization of Egypt in the Eighteenth Dynasty. I am deeply in debt to the authorities there uncited, still more to the busy friends and colleagues who have patiently read my book or sections of it in manuscript. John D. Cooney, curator of the Department of Ancient Art of the Brooklyn Museum; Dows Dunham, curator emeritus of the Department of Egyptian Art of the Museum of Fine Arts, Boston; Walter Federn; and the late William C. Hayes of the Department of Egyptian Art of the Metropolitan Museum of Art, New York, have all helped me with suggestion and correction, though none of them is responsible for my sins of omission or commission. In addition, I am most grateful to Miss Mary B. Cairns of the Museum of Fine Arts, Boston, for her painstaking copy of an untidy original manuscript, to Miss Suzanne E. Chapman of the same institution for her skillful adaptation from several sources of a sketch map of Egypt, and to the Oriental Institute of the University of Chicago for permission to use the plan of the West Bank of Thebes in the Eighteenth Dynasty, first published in Uvo Hölscher's *The Temples of the Eighteenth Dynasty* (Chicago, 1939), 66 (Excavations of Medinet Habu II, Oriental Institute *Publications XLI*).

ELIZABETH RIEFSTAHL

Essex, Massachusetts
January 27, 1964

Contents

Thebes

IN THE TIME OF
AMUNHOTEP III

If any reader of this work of mine suffers nausea as he gets to the end, he is not to blame me, but himself. Before he ever began to read it, he knew quite well how little renown I have for scholarship, and it is only his own fault if he has stuck to it to the last page.

AMALAR OF METZ,
INTERPRETATION OF THE CANON OF THE MASS,
AS TRANSLATED IN CAROLINGIAN PORTRAITS,
BY ELEANOR SHIPLEY DUCKETT (ANN ARBOR,
UNIVERSITY OF MICHIGAN PRESS, 1962).

CHAPTER ONE

Thebes Enters History

A HAPHAZARD JUMBLE of undistinguished shops and dwellings, with here a hotel set in the welcome green of a garden, there a gaunt ruin, still noble in decay; a stagnant, provincial town, fraying out into dusty villages and fields that offer a precarious living in exchange for toil from dawn to dusk—such is Thebes today. Whatever exotic charm it may have shared a few years past with many another sleepy, Oriental town is fast disappearing under slick, modern improvements for the attraction of tourists. All winter long, sight-seers whiz in motor cars from monument to monument. No more, the shadowy walk in the cool of the evening on the tree-shaded road along the Nile to visit Karnak by moonlight. That road is brilliantly lighted, and a pavilion for dispensing snacks to the hungry visitor guards the approach to the great temple. In the necropolis across the river, even the austere Valley of the Kings has been robbed of its mystery. The desert track leading to it has been widened and leveled and flanked by light poles so that the hurried tourist may usefully employ his evening hours in visiting the tombs of the pharaohs. The inevitable snack bar has been erected in the very midst of the valley, and it has been announced that escalators will be installed in the deep-hewn corridors that lead to the hidden burial chambers of the kings.

In summer the town that was once Thebes and the vast

necropolis opposite it lapse into somnolence under the hot sun. The tourists have fled; the great hotels are closed. The archaeologists who have busied themselves in seeking out and recording the past have carried off their notes to cooler climates. The *fellahin* have harvested their crops and cluster in their villages, waiting for the rising Nile to flood and fertilize their fields for new sowing. In tiny settlements in and around the ancient tombs, a few men lazily chip away at bits of limestone, making *antikas* for next winter's credulous visitors.

The quiet of long, sunny days is broken by the buzzing of innumerable flies, the crying of children, and quick-flaring noisy quarrels. In Luxor a gramophone whines a modern tune into the street. In the necropolis the valley sometimes echoes to the ululating wails of women mourning a death or to a shrill recitative of the virtues of the departed, addressed to the four quarters of heaven. On the way to the Moslem burying ground near Karnak village, a cortege of men, headed by a band blaring alien music, conducts the green-turbaned coffin of a notable to the grave. To the hardly recognizable yet not inappropriate melody of "The Wearin' o' the Green," they go, now fast, now slow, in accordance with the unvoiced protest of the dead man against leaving this fair world, and finally quicken to irreverent quickstep when the cemetery comes into view.

At night the shadows are alive with the yapping and howling of half-starved village dogs and the antiphonic barking of jackals that prowl among the ruins. The din only serves to make the silence and vast emptiness more felt, to heighten the impression that Thebes is today dead and populated by ghosts.

An Egyptian of the Eighteenth Dynasty would not recognize in the tawdry Thebes of the present his beautiful, bustling city, which once rose on the banks of the Nile to become for all time a symbol of wealth and grandeur and power. He would not even recognize the name by which we call it—a name given to it by the Greeks, perhaps because some local epithet sounded to their alien ears like the name of the Boeotian Thebes. The Egyptians named their city "Waset," "the Scepter," after the nome, or province, in which it sprang up. Sometimes they referred to it as the "City of Amun," its great god, but more often they called it simply "The City." "She is called 'The City,' " says a late New Kingdom hymn in her praise; "all the others are under her shadow, to magnify themselves through her"; and when Ramesses II built his new capital in the Delta, the highest praise that could be given to it was that it was "a fair throne . . . after the pattern of Thebes."

Various sections of Thebes had their own names. The great temple of the god Amun at present-day Karnak, which grew to be a town within a town, was known as Ipet-Isut, perhaps to be translated as "Most-Select-of-Places," and that of the same god at Luxor, as the Southern Opet, that is, the Southern Sanctuary (harem). The necropolis, itself a thriving city of the living in the service of the dead, was frequently referred to as "Opposite-Its-Lord," that is, across the river from the abode of Amun; sometimes it was just "West-of-the-City."

According to Strabo, who saw Thebes shortly before the time of Christ when it had been reduced to a collection of villages and a Roman garrison was quartered in the ruins of the Southern Sanctuary, the city in its prime stretched for nine miles along the Nile. It probably included many suburbs, such as nearby Medamud, the abode of the war god Montu. The ruins of his temple there date from the time of the

Ptolemies, but among them are many reused blocks from earlier temples, and they cover a recently excavated shrine that is apparently of great antiquity.

Thebes proper could boast of no such antiquity. Although a poet of the Nineteenth Dynasty voiced the claim that The City had existed from the beginning of time, its origins and those of its god Amun, who became and for many centuries remained the state god of Egypt, are lost in obscurity. Other great sacred cities of Egypt—Heliopolis, Memphis, Abydos—and many lesser ones go back to the earliest dynasties and even to the shadowy times before history. Not so Thebes. It is possible that a few poor villages may lie under modern dwellings, but the earliest evidence of occupation of the site is provided by a scant half-dozen shabby burials of the late Old Kingdom, among them those of nomarchs, or governors, of the Scepter province, who found their last resting place in the necropolis that was later to become one of the richest and most populous the world has ever known.

The city first appeared in history when a group of enterprising Egyptians settled there toward the end of the third millennium B.C. and made it their headquarters for the reunification of Egypt, which had fallen apart during the years of misgovernment and confusion that followed the collapse of the Old Kingdom. This was not the first time—nor was it to be the last—that the unification of Egypt had been accomplished by vigorous men of the South. At the very beginning of history, the country had first been brought under a single rule by an Upper Egyptian king known in legend as Menes. The dynasty he founded had its origin at Hierakonpolis, far up the Nile, and had established a seat at Thinis, near Abydos, which remained a sacred place to the end of pharaonic history; but it was from Memphis, near the apex of the Delta, that he ruled the united land. After his reign Egypt flourished for nearly a thousand years before the administration slipped out of the feeble hands of Pepi II, the last effectual ruler of the Sixth Dynasty.

Pepi II, who enjoyed the longest reign in the history of the world, had lived too long. He came to the throne as a child of six and held the scepter for about ninety-four years. Even before his advent the government had begun to weaken. Its resources of men and wealth had been squandered in grandiose construction—temples, tombs, and the greatest of the pyramids. There is, moreover (as recent research has indicated), the possibility that toward the end of the Old Kingdom a change of climate such as is known to have taken place in contemporary Europe and Palestine may have affected the economy of Egypt. Successive years of low Nile or perhaps a devastating earthquake accompanied by famine and pestilence may have contributed to an unrest that grew beyond bounds, resulting in what amounted to civil war. A strong ruler might possibly have prevented the final collapse. But the aging King, hedged about with luxury and ritual, lived more and more remote in his palace and allowed the power to slip into the hands of hereditary nobles. By the time of his death, these ambitious and greedy provincial governors had tired of sending their wealth and produce for the enrichment of the capital at Memphis and had established themselves in their provinces as princes independent of central authority.

Small as the population of Egypt must have been, Memphis had grown disproportionately until it constituted a drain upon the whole land. Crowded into a narrow strip hedged in by desert was a multitude of persons who lived on the bounty of the King. There was the palace, teeming with courtiers, harem women, servants, and slaves. There were the mansions of great officials, often related to the King, with swarms of progeny and attendants. There were the government offices with many employees and the temples thronged with clergy and attendant personnel. The great necropolis at the desert's edge employed hundreds. The pyramid temples all had their priests and acolytes for the cults of dead pharaohs. Villages of officiants and workmen had arisen among the tombs, and a small army of men had been impressed for labor in the quarries that supplied fine white limestone for building the city of the dead.

All of these persons (and the list is far from complete) were paid in kind; and when revenues failed, they were not paid at all. The contrast between rich and poor had undoubtedly always been great in Memphis; and now, as the power gradually slipped out of the hands of the King, the poor, whose hands had built the city, were reduced from a bare living to starvation. It has been suggested, with some plausibility, that the final debacle of the Old Kingdom was marked by a rebellion of the proletariat when starving workers desperately turned to violence and pillage. However that may be, the successor of Pepi II ruled only briefly before the government collapsed and the country was reduced to chaos.

Sir Alan Gardiner has published a papyrus under the title *The Admonitions of an Egyptian Sage,* which purports to be a record of those troubled times made by an Egyptian named Ipuwer, who had lived through them. "A few lawless men," says Ipuwer, "have ventured to despoil the land of its kingship." He goes on to report how raiding foreigners had ventured into Egypt. Brother had turned against brother. Lawlessness reigned; records were destroyed, palaces sacked and burned, tombs violated: "What the pyramid concealed," says the sage, "is become empty." Craftsmen no longer plied their trades; crops failed through lack of labor or were destroyed; famine and plague, pillage and carnage were universal. "Squalor is throughout the land. There are none whose clothes are white in these times. . . . The poor have become rich, and the possessor of property has become one who has nothing." Whether this papyrus is an authentic record or not, it conveys a vivid picture of what might have happened—and what could happen—in Egypt when the central administration broke down.

Egypt was not an easy country to control. While it possessed almost unparalleled natural defenses against aggression and influence from the outside world, it was also divided by nature into parts that made for disunity. There was always, as there is today, an Upper and a Lower Egypt, the former consisting of the long, narrow valley of the Nile, and the latter, of the broad flatlands through which the river fans out to reach the sea. The pharaohs showed this duality in their titles. From the very beginning down to the time of the Roman emperors, they were kings of "Upper and Lower Egypt" or of the "Two Lands," never simply kings of Egypt.

It required a strong government to hold the two parts together. The narrow valley of Upper Egypt stretched southward for nearly six hundred miles to the First Cataract, where the river narrowed to rush in a series of rapids through granite gorges, which formed a natural defense against invasion from the south. On the west, at the edge of the level valley carved out by the Nile, rose an escarpment of cliffs, beyond which lay the wide plateau of the Western, or Libyan, Desert,

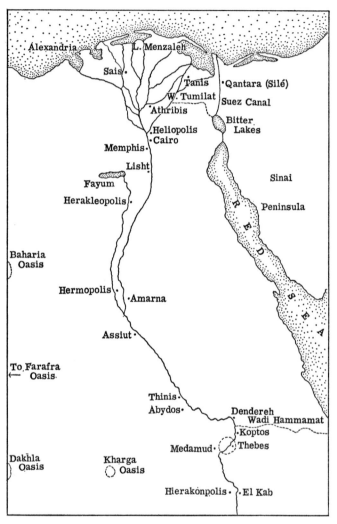

Lower Egypt

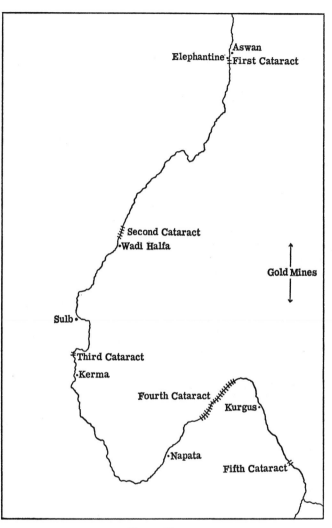

Upper Egypt

sparsely inhabited by nomad tribes. Today this desert is water-less and almost entirely lacking in vegetation. In antiquity, however, parts of it provided a meager pasturage for the flocks of nomads and food and shelter for the wild beasts which kings and nobles loved to hunt. Along it were strung at wide intervals fertile oases, many days' travel from the Nile Valley.

To the east of that valley was the formidable Eastern, or Arabian, Desert, with high, rugged mountain ranges pierced by dry watercourses made in times beyond memory. Through one of these deep-cut ravines, the Wadi Hammamat, lay the shortest route to the Red Sea, an ancient caravan road leading from Koptos, some thirty miles north of Thebes, to a point near the modern Kosseir. Along it were quarries that supplied hard stones, so prized for statues and sarcophagi, and from the Red Sea coast were accessible the incense ports of Africa. The Eastern Desert was rich in gold and semiprecious stones, and also, inhospitable as it was, it offered rare water holes and wells, which made life possible for a scanty population. Por-tions of it are still sparsely peopled today, in part by dwindling remnants of tribes perhaps descended from the same ancestors whose more daring progeny fled the gradually desiccating deserts as early as paleolithic times to settle in the fertile, animal-haunted jungle of the Nile Valley.

The sedentary Egyptians of pharaonic times had entirely forgotten their remote desert heritage. They feared the "Red Land," as they called the desert (in contradistinction to the "Black Land" fed and watered by the Nile), and imagined it haunted by demons and mythical monsters. Yet they braved it for the sake of treasure as early as predynastic times. Inscrip-tions carved on the rocks of the perilous route to the Red Sea tell of expeditions that followed it since the time of the Old

Kingdom and down into the Roman Period. Among others, an official named Henu records how he traveled from Koptos late in the third millennium before Christ and built and dispatched a ship to Punt, on the Somali coast, to bring back to the king "fresh myrrh from the sheiks over the Red Land." He dug wells along the route and boasted, "I made the road a river and the Red Land a tract of fields, for I gave . . . two jars of water and twenty loaves to each man every day. . . . Never was done the like of this by any king's confidant. . . . I did this for the majesty of my lord, because he so much loved me." The Vizier Amenemhet of a slightly later reign inscribed the account of his journey to the "august highland" with an army of men, "the choicest of the whole land," including miners, artists, stonecutters, and scribes, to hew out a sarcophagus for the king, "an everlasting reminder." He proudly claimed not to have lost a man, not even so much as an ass; but this was due to the favor of the god Min, protector of the desert, granted in return for royal piety.

The fertility of Upper Egypt depended entirely on the annual inundation of the Nile, which watered and fed the rainless valley. If the flood failed, there was famine. At a very early period the inhabitants of the valley learned that a certain amount of cooperation was needed for the building of dykes and canals and irrigation ditches to control and husband the waters; and it is perhaps at least partly for this reason that throughout history the rulers of the Two Lands were frequently Upper Egyptians, schooled in such co-operation.

Lower Egypt presented a different problem. There the question was primarily one of drainage, for the Nile Delta, that great triangle anciently watered by seven branches of the river instead of two as today, was rarely dry; and it enjoyed, moreover, a limited amount of winter rainfall, particularly in the northern portion. It was—and is—the most fertile part of Egypt. At its apex, toward the south, were the famous early cities, Heliopolis and Memphis. On its western fringe were fine grazing lands, coveted by Libyan herdsmen. For the rest, a scant population of primitive hunters and fishermen roamed its marshes, except where scattered, ancient towns rose on mounds or ridges above the swamplands. These towns were surrounded by fields and vineyards, but during the inundation they were, as Diodorus tells us, like islands in a broad sea. Because of the nature of the terrain, which makes archaeological investigation difficult, indeed often impossible, we are very poorly informed about the early history of the Delta. Even the locations of some of the cities named in ancient records have not been determined. We know, however, that certain important centers were in the Eastern region, strategically located near the routes to Asia.

The principal ways through the Delta to the Near East were few and difficult. The northern shore was all but harborless and was protected on the land side by morasses and brackish lakes and on the sea by hidden sand bars. The ancient sea route to Syria was probably chiefly by way of the Tanitic branch of the Nile, a branch that has now dwindled to a stream, which loses itself in the marshes of Lake Menzaleh, but that was once, with the vanished Pelusiac branch to the east of it, one of the main arteries of Egypt. The principal land route led by way of the modern Kantara. Another route, through the Wadi Tumilat, branched to the north to join the Kantara road and to the south, skirting the Bitter Lakes, to reach the head of the Gulf of Suez, from which the turquoise mines of Sinai and the incense ports of the Red Sea were accessible by sea. All of these routes were arduous and fraught with danger, but from very early times the Egyptians dared them in search of luxuries which their own land could not supply.

During the Old Kingdom bold navigators, much as they hated and feared the "Great Green," as they called the sea, sailed to Byblos on the Syrian coast to bring back wood from the forests of Lebanon for furniture and coffins and for the embellishment of temples, journeyed on the Red Sea to the incense-land of Punt, and worked their way south along the Nile beyond the Second Cataract for the sake of ivory, ebony, and gold. Nevertheless, the people of the early dynasties, secure in their country so admirably fortified by nature, refused to recognize that anything existed beyond the Two Lands. To them, Egypt was the world; nothing that lay beyond counted.

It was undoubtedly a matter for surprise and consternation that neighboring peoples dared to take advantage of the confusion following the death of Pepi II to invade the weakened country and even to settle there. Such invasions, though on a modest scale—perhaps little more than raids of nomad bands from the hungry deserts to the east and the west—added to the turmoil of what we call the First Intermediate Period, which lasted for nearly two hundred years. During this time Egypt became much as it had been during predynastic times, a series of petty principalities whose rulers squabbled with one another for power. While most of these rulers were no better than robber barons, some of them, as is shown by inscriptions in their tombs, assumed the epithets of royalty.

Not long after the collapse of the Sixth Dynasty, a dynasty

of kings called by modern historians the "Herakleopolitans," gained a precarious control of part of Egypt from their capital at Nen Nysut (the Greek Herakleopolis and the modern Ahnasya), which lies some fifty miles south of the capital of the Old Kingdom pharaohs at Memphis. Reputedly by means of a reign of terror, the first king of the dynasty established himself in Memphis and Middle Egypt. From this foothold his successors, after a long struggle, subdued the Delta, expelling the Asiatic invaders and reopening trade with the Syrian coast. But they never entirely succeeded in subduing the South. Especially the Theban region, where the family that was to cause their downfall was growing in strength, remained impatient of control.

The earliest princes of this family, most of them rather confusingly called Intef, were nomarchs of the Scepter province and nominally subject to the kings of Herakleopolis. Their successors, also usually Intefs, gave up all pretense of being subject to anybody and established themselves at Thebes as kings of Upper and Lower Egypt. These first kings of the Eleventh Dynasty, Montuhotep I and Intefs I, II, and III, had small claim to that grandiose title, though they gradually gained control of the Nile Valley to the southern borders of Egypt and began to push the Herakleopolitan kings northward. It was not until about 2040 B.C. that a king called Nebhepetre Montuhotep II finally routed the Herakleopolitans and reunited the Two Lands. Under him and his successor, Seankhkare Montuhotep III, Thebes began, if only in a small way, to be a city.

Little is left of Eleventh Dynasty structures there, and only traces of the burials of the kings of that dynasty survive in the gravelly plain opposite Karnak. There is evidence that these pharaohs erected a temple somewhere in the neighborhood of Karnak to Montu, a god of obscure origins who perhaps gained his reputation as a war god through his association with his warlike devotees and namesakes, the Montuhoteps, whose name signifies "Montu-Is-Pleased." There seems also to have been at Karnak a small structure dedicated to Amun. The latter god, however, was as yet little known. In the first of the fine buildings in the necropolis, the beautiful mortuary temple of Nebhepetre Montuhotep II at Deir el Bahri, the King boasts that he is "Beloved of Montu, Lord of Thebes," and but scanty reference to Amun survives from there or from anywhere in inscriptions of the Eleventh Dynasty.

It was not until the Twelfth Dynasty, when a new family took over the power, that Amun began to come into his own. Four of the rulers of this dynasty, including the first one, were named Amunemhet, "Amun-Is-Foremost," and the god's temple, which was to become the vastest and richest in the history of Egypt, was securely established at Karnak. While later kings, rebuilding and adding to the temple, obscured or destroyed most of the Twelfth Dynasty structures, modern archaeology has rescued almost intact a peripteral limestone pavilion erected for the jubilee of the second king of that dynasty, Senwosret (Sesostris) I, which had been used as fill in the monumental gateway later built by Amunhotep III of the New Kingdom. This little pavilion is, in its simplicity, one of the most beautiful buildings of the Egyptian past; its walls, for which the fine stone was imported from far down the Nile, are decorated with delicately perfect reliefs, showing the King with his divine associate Amun.

There is not much else left at Karnak to recall the great

kings of the Twelfth Dynasty, though scattered blocks indicate that the temples they erected there and elsewhere in the Theban district were of a splendor rivaling that of the New Kingdom. These kings, Thebans as they were, did not neglect Thebes nor its god Amun, but quite logically found Egypt easier to govern from the ancient administrative center at the apex of the Delta, where the Two Lands joined. They ruled from It-towy in the vicinity of Memphis and were buried nearby at the desert's edge in richly equipped pyramids that sought to emulate the mighty pyramid-tombs of Old Kingdom pharaohs.

Certain of their officials, however, among them some who had followed their royal masters to the north but wished to be buried in their homeland of Upper Egypt, built tombs cut into the cliffs of the Theban necropolis, and the kings themselves erected statues in their own likenesses at Medamud and Karnak and in the funerary temple of Nebhepetre Montuhotep, from whom they claimed descent (probably with scant justification, for the first king of the Twelfth Dynasty, probably the onetime Vizier Amunemhet mentioned above, seems not to have been of direct royal ancestry).

The Amunemhets and Senwosrets of the Twelfth Dynasty were remarkable rulers. It needs only a glance at their portraits, which are among the most individualistic Egypt ever produced, to recognize that they were men of intelligence and power. They were confronted with the difficult task of restoring the prestige of the throne, so completely demolished after the fall of the Old Kingdom and never entirely reestablished by the parochially minded Thebans of the Eleventh Dynasty; and while the Twelfth Dynasty kings never quite attained the unquestioned supremacy of the divine rulers of the Old

Kingdom, they ruled wisely and well. One of their problems was the rebuilding of a class of literate clerks and officials, so necessary for the administration of the land. With this end in view, they fostered a propagandist literature, in which the profession of scribe was extolled at the expense of all other occupations—a literature that was to be cherished and preserved by the mammoth bureaucracy of the New Kingdom.

Among the accomplishments of the Twelfth Dynasty was the reorganization of the administrative system through a redistribution of the nomes, or provinces, in an attempt to bring and keep the feudal governors under control. During that period also, the office of the vizier, or prime minister, to whom much of the administration of the country was necessarily delegated by the active kings, increased in importance, and the manifold duties of that functionary were established in detail. The pharaohs undertook many public works. They attempted for the first time in history some drainage of the Delta and began to realize the possibilities of the fertile oasis nearest to the Nile Valley, the Fayum, with its great ancient lake, not far upriver from Memphis. In the South they cleared and improved a canal that had been built by Merenre I, the predecessor of Pepi II, to by-pass the First Cataract and open the Nile south of it to navigation. There was even a legend in later Egypt that one of the Senwosrets had built the canal linking the Nile Valley with the Red Sea and that a Senwosret had rounded the Arabian Peninsula to reach the borders of Mesopotamia. Such legends, still current in the time of the Greek tourists who came to wonder at the decaying splendor of Egypt, indicate in what honor the great rulers of the Middle Kingdom were held down to the very end of the ancient civilization.

Indeed, later Egyptians looked back on the Twelfth Dynasty as the classical period of Egyptian culture. Its literature set a standard for future generations—much of it survives only in the form of exercises laboriously copied by schoolboys of the New Kingdom; its language was preserved in religious ritual long after it had ceased to be the spoken or written language of the country (and it is, incidentally, the language first learned by students of the present day); its art was held in such esteem that it was taken as a model, especially—and with a fidelity often confusing to modern art historians—by artists who flourished during the brief renaissance of the seventh and sixth centuries before Christ.

Under the rulers of the Twelfth Dynasty, Egypt prospered for more than two hundred years. Then followed a second period of division and disorder. The strength of the ruling family diminished, and rival factions competed for the throne. Without profiting from the experience of their predecessors, the pharoahs had vied with one another and exhausted the treasury in elaborate building. Their greed for foreign luxuries had led them into expansion beyond the borders of Egypt. While earlier rulers had been, on the whole, content to keep the borders guarded against aggression and open for commerce, Twelfth Dynasty expeditions followed the Nile far into Nubia, beyond the Third Cataract, building forts along the way and establishing garrisons and colonies to control trade in the products of the African hinterland. In the north, Egyptian merchants not only sailed to the ports of the Syrian coast, but penetrated the interior, leaving behind them monuments testifying to their presence.

Although Senwosret III is known to have made one military expedition into Palestine, taking the city of Sichem, relationships between Egypt and the countries to the east seem, on the whole, to have been on a basis of diplomacy rather than of warfare. Rulers exchanged gifts, and there was apparently a free coming and going of merchants and caravans. While new fortifications guarded the main routes from the East, there was so little premonition of danger that the close of the Twelfth Dynasty found the Delta subject to a "peaceful penetration" of tribes from overseas. Weak rulers of the later Twelfth Dynasty permitted the power to slip into the hands of their viziers, for whom they became little better than puppets. As the dynasty fell apart, aliens seem to have wormed their way even into the palace, for among the kings of the Thirteenth Dynasty were some whose names betray a foreign origin.

These kings tried in vain to hold the country together. Not only did Egypt once more break up into a series of petty kingdoms, but among these was a principality set up at Avaris in the Eastern Delta (probably the present Tanis) by a group of Asiatic invaders who gradually possessed the land. These invaders were called in later times "Hyksos"—a word often translated as "Shepherd Kings" but meaning simply "rulers of foreign countries." Other than the fact that they came from the East, nothing much is known about them, though it seems possible that they were an agglomeration of tribes pushed westward by unrest in Hither Asia. In the state of disunity prevailing in the Two Lands, they met with little resistance. Not long after their rise, they conquered Memphis, and they ultimately pushed south as far as Aswan; but their hold on Upper Egypt remained always tenuous.

While later Theban rulers of the New Kingdom made great case of the wickedness of the "hateful Asiatics," the

Hyksos were probably not much worse than any occupying force, ancient or modern. Pillage and outrage and sporadic clashes of arms undoubtedly occurred, but the invaders managed to retain a hold over all of Egypt for well over a century, and in that length of time some basis for a relatively peaceful coexistence must have been established. Indeed, the Hyksos seem to have found among the Egyptians willing collaborators who later met with retribution at the hands of Kamose, the predecessor and brother of the Theban king who ultimately vanquished them. He recorded: "I hacked up their towns and set fire to their dwellings, so that they were made into red tells [desert mounds] eternally, because of the damage they had done in Egypt when they gave themselves to serve the Asiatics, forsaking Egypt, their mistress."

Since the Hyksos had scant culture of their own, they readily adopted Egyptian arts and customs, even to some extent Egyptian religion. The new rulers took over the titulary of Egyptian kings: like the latter, they were "Sons of Re," the ancient Egyptian solar god from whom all pharaohs claimed descent. In their capital at Avaris in the Delta, they set up their own thunder god, who was identified with the Egyptian god Seth. Sparse remains indicate that they added to and embellished certain Egyptian temples, while despoiling others. Though what little survives from the Hyksos period in the way of art and architecture shows a decline in skill, extant papyri indicate that the ancient learning continued undiminished in the temples.

If the arts were not their forte, the conquerors were able, nevertheless, to make important contributions to Egyptian culture. Besides introducing new weapons and improved methods of warfare, they brought with them mechanical inventions such as the *shaduf*, or sweep, an aid to irrigation still in use, and probably the vertical loom, which makes its first appearance in Theban tomb paintings of the early New Kingdom. They are also credited with having introduced into Egypt the horse and the wheeled vehicle, which were to play so prominent a part in the military annals of the Empire.

There is reason to believe that the horse may have been previously known, though only as a rarity. There is no evidence that it was used to any extent by the Hyksos in their conquest of Egypt, and whatever importance horses and chariots may have come to have in future Asiatic campaigns, they remained little more than prestige items in the homeland for centuries to come. Kings of the Eighteenth Dynasty and later had their stables. Princes of the Thutmosid line vaunted their skill in taming and handling steeds "fleet as the wind," but horses were not bred in Egypt; they were expensive, imported luxuries, almost entirely reserved for royal use. It is significant that horse burials of the pharaonic period are excessively rare—the only known one of indisputably early date is that in the tomb of Senenmut, the onetime favorite of Queen Hatshepsut, and such chariots as have survived have come exclusively from the tombs of kings or members of royal families.

Wheeled vehicles were of little use in a canal- and ditch-gridded land. As Herodotos noted (II, 108), Egypt, from the time of "Sesostris" (to whom he credited the irrigation works), "albeit a level land, could use no horses and carts, by reason of the canals being so many and going every way." A very few representations of wheeled carts drawn by oxen are known, but evidently such means of transport were rarely employed. The chariot, light as a modern sandcart, was chiefly the plaything of princes who hunted over desert steppes, the equipage used by kings and nobles on brief processional ways, the vehicle of royal couriers, working in relays. "Come to thy sister quickly," says a New Kingdom love song, "like the royal envoy whose lord is impatient for his message . . . an envoy for whom all the stables have been requisitioned. He has horses at the resting places. The chariot stands harnessed and ready. Nor is there any breathing space for him upon the road." (After Alan H. Gardiner, *The Chester Beatty Papyri, No. I* [Oxford, 1931], 35.)

It seems remarkable that the Egyptians, so apt in skills, never grasped the full implication of the wheel: it remained for later peoples to reintroduce the wheel in the forms of the pulley and the *sakkia*, that great water wheel which today makes the Nile Valley echo to its creaking. And the Egyptians never became equestrians. There are isolated representations of mounted grooms and orderlies, but no king or notable is ever pictured on horseback, no lesser person astride a donkey. The ass remained a beast of burden, the boat or the litter, the means of transport for those too proud to walk.

In spite of what they brought and despite clumsy attempts at conciliation, the Hyksos shared the usual fate of occupying forces: though sometimes tolerated, they were never entirely accepted. Indeed, there seems to have arisen in Egypt under their rule the first feeling of national unity. Certainly, for the first time in their history, Egyptians became aware of the false security in which they had lived for many centuries.

Long before the Hyksos were expelled, independent principalities in Middle and Upper Egypt had broken away from their control. Among these, as might be expected, was a Theban kingdom, whose leaders began open rebellion against the next-to-the-last king of the Hyksos, Apepi; and as he vainly appealed for help to the Prince of Kush (Nubia), they drove him almost to Memphis. This victory was celebrated on two stelae set up by the Theban King Kamose in the temple of Amun at Karnak. Under Kamose's brother and successor, Ahmose, the Hyksos were finally driven out of Egypt and even followed into southern Palestine, where they were given the *coup de grace*; and the Eighteenth Dynasty, with Ahmose as king and Thebes as the capital of reunited Egypt, was launched on the way to becoming an empire.

One of the first things that Ahmose turned his hand to, once the country was at peace, was the reconstruction and re-equipment of the temples of the gods, neglected or looted or destroyed during the Hyksos occupation. Chief honor was paid to the god with whom subsequent history of the dynasty was to be closely associated—Amun, or Amun-Re, as he should now be known, for at some time along his rise to national importance, he had become identified with the powerful sun god of Heliopolis. A fragmentary stela records some of the riches heaped by Ahmose upon his divine protector at the temple of Karnak—chaplets of gold with rosettes of real lapis lazuli, necklaces of gold and silver adorned with lapis lazuli and malachite, countless libation vases and offering tables of gold and silver, jars of pink granite filled with ointment, a harp of ebony, gold, and silver, sphinxes of silver, and a barge of the "best new cedar," in which the god could make his voyages.

The immediate successor of Ahmose, Amunhotep I, came to the throne as a minor, under the regency of his mother, Queen Ahmose-Nofretari. Although he ruled for twenty years, he remains a shadowy figure. There are hints that he consolidated Egypt's position in Palestine and successfully quelled a rebellion in Nubia. Otherwise, little is known about him; but he and his mother came to be worshiped as founders of the dynasty and tutelary deities of the Theban necropolis, where they were revered for many hundreds of years.

Amunhotep I and his successors, Thutmose I and Thutmose II, added to and embellished the abode of Amun at Karnak. Amunhotep I built there a limestone structure ornamented with reliefs of great delicacy and erected as a repository for the sacred bark of Amun a little alabaster shrine, which foretells the refinement of decoration characteristic of the Eighteenth Dynasty. He also ordered for himself a modest tomb in a desert *wadi* not far from the entrance to the Valley of the Kings, where his royal successors were to be buried. So far as is known, he was the first of the Eighteenth Dynasty kings to hide away his tomb and build a mortuary temple at the edge of cultivation, remote from his burial place.

An architect named Ineni who served under Amunhotep I and lived to see his successor on the throne records in his tomb at Thebes some of the works which he executed for his royal masters. At the behest of Thutmose I, he threw a wall about the sacred precinct of Amun and built a great pillared hall at its western end. He also supervised the erection of monumental gateways, or pylons, for the same king. The first, called "Amun-Mighty-in-Wealth," had between its flanking towers a "great door made of Asiatic copper, whereon was the Divine Shadow, inlaid with gold." Before it were flagstaves made of tall cedars brought from Lebanon and tipped with electrum to catch the rays of the sun. The pylon still stands, though stripped of its color, its inlaid doors, and its lofty staves with their flying pennants. Ineni further records the building for Thutmose I of the first of the royal tombs in the Valley of the Kings. "I inspected," he says, "the excavation of the cliff-tomb of His Majesty—alone, no one seeing, no one hearing." Futile precaution, for in spite of all secrecy, Thutmose's burial and those of most of his successors were robbed and the bodies of the deified kings profaned before the New Kingdom came to its undistinguished end. The very location of his valley temple is unknown.

Thutmose I was not the son of his predecessor. He may have been distantly related to the royal family on his father's side, but his mother was a commoner; and his claim to the throne was cemented by marriage to a princess of the blood, another Ahmose, who was probably a sister of Amunhotep I. A soldier by training, this first of the Thutmosids foreshadowed the exploits of his more famous grandson, Thutmose III, the Conqueror. He progressed into Nubia beyond the Fourth Cataract and tightened Egypt's control over the southland. An inscription of his on a quartz rock at present-day Kurgus indicates that Egyptian influence was felt almost to the Fifth Cataract, on the borders of negro Africa. In Asia he carried Egyptian conquest to the Euphrates, defeating the troublesome prince of Mitanni, who threatened Syria from the East; and he designated the great eastern river (flowing, to Egyptian wonderment, in the "wrong" direction) as the boundary of Egypt. Though this was an anticipation of fact, the seventeen-year reign of Thutmose I carried Egypt far toward the royal aim of Asiatic conquest.

His son, Thutmose II, was little more than a boy when he acceded to the throne; but since he was born of a minor wife, he had already been married to his half-sister Hatshepsut in order to support his claim to the crown. Though he was sickly and died before he reached the prime of life, the affairs of the kingdom ran smoothly under his rule. This may have been due in part to his formidable queen, whose name has come down to us as that of a remarkable, if somewhat unscrupulous, woman. She was left as regent for the King's minor son, Thutmose III, whom he had named as his heir. Like his father and grandfather before him, Thutmose III was not the offspring of the "Great Royal Wife," but was born of a secondary wife named Isis. His title to the throne was confirmed (or so he claimed many years later) by a divine oracle, and may have been further legitimized (though this is unproved) by marriage to a princess of irreproachable descent, his half-sister, the daughter and only child of Thutmose II and Hatshepsut. Long after he was of an age to rule, however, Thutmose III was king in name only.

Having tasted of power in the early years of her stepson's minority, Hatshepsut seized and held the reins of government in her own capable hands. Her ambition—and her imagination—knew no bounds. Supported by a group of strong courtiers, she pretended (as did other rulers) to be the offspring of the god Amun-Re, who had appeared to her mother in the guise of her earthly father, Thutmose I. She claimed, moreover, to have been crowned by the latter as his successor, completely ignoring her half-brother–husband, who had ruled as king for eighteen years. Not content with being queen, she had herself pictured as king, in male dress and wearing the false beard reserved for gods and divine rulers. Her texts frequently show a curious, though perhaps inevitable, confusion of gender, for in them "she" is mentioned as the "good god," the "Horus," the "Son of Re."

There is no doubt that Hatshepsut was able—and had able

advisers. The internal affairs of the country ran smoothly, and Egypt flourished under her rule. The land was at peace, tribute poured into the treasury from the regions subdued by her predecessors, and trade proceeded unhampered along the routes which they had made safe. Much of the wealth thus poured into Egypt was expended for the glory of the gods, for the Egyptians were always, as Herodotos remarked a millennium later, "beyond measure religious." Under the direction of her Overseer of Works, Senenmut, Hatshepsut restored or added to many temples, but she reserved her best efforts for Thebes. Her proudest accomplishments were the two great obelisks which she erected in the Karnak temple of her father Amun and the expedition she sent to Punt, on the Somali coast, to bring back incense for the pleasure of his nostrils and living frankincense trees for the temple grove at Deir el Bahri. These deeds she recorded on the walls of her funerary temple in West-of-the-City, where reliefs show the transport of the monolithic obelisks from the granite quarries at Aswan, some 130 miles up the Nile, and picture the ships of her incense-bearing fleet and the strange lands and peoples seen by her emissaries on the far-off shores of the Red Sea.

The vaunted obelisks, whose tips "pierced the sky and illumined the Two Lands like the disk of the sun," have long since been shattered, but one of another pair she erected still stands in Karnak at the end of the pillared court built by her father, which she partly demolished to make place for them; and her temple at Deir el Bahri, rising against the cliff, battered as it is and deprived of its ambient groves and gardens, remains one of the most impressive monuments of Egypt. Inspired by the neighboring Eleventh Dynasty temple of Nebhepetre Montuhotep, but much larger, it ascends in two deep colonnaded terraces approached by monumental ramps, to dominate the Valley. Below the terraces are the remains of a walled forecourt, and at their summit, cut in the cliff, is the principal sanctuary, dedicated to Amun. The temple also includes chapels to the goddess Hathor and to the jackal-headed god Anubis, both custodians of the necropolis, as well as shrines for the cult of Hatshepsut herself and of her father, Thutmose I, who was venerated by the workers of the necropolis long after she had been forgotten.

Majestic as it is, the temple gives an impression of lightness, in striking contrast with the solid dignity of many Theban monuments; and more than any other architectural work of the Egyptian past, it seems an inevitable part of its natural setting. The delicate reliefs with which it is adorned show a freedom, a subtly feminine charm that is lacking in the previous more restrained and hieratic work. They have an almost lyrical quality, and it has been remarked that something of their poetry has crept into the very inscriptions that supplement the pictured scenes.

The Queen is represented on every wall. Her divine birth, her coronation, her exploits, her worship of the gods are all depicted. Small wonder that Thutmose III, when her death finally released him from subjugation, had her likenesses hacked away and her name overlaid with his own or that of her father. He overthrew and buried statues showing the Queen in the form of Osiris, along with other sculptures depicting her in her regal dress and a long series of royal sphinxes that had flanked a broad processional way leading to the Nile. The temple itself, dedicated as it was to Amun, was spared, only to suffer further mutilation a century later, when the "heretic king," Akhenaten, caused the name of Amun to be effaced from it.

In the shadowy background of Hatshepsut's reign, one senses intrigues and counterintrigues. It is more than possible that Hatshepsut owed much of her reputation as an able administrator to the group of courtiers who found it to their advantage to use her as a willing tool. Chief among them was her favorite, Senenmut, a man of humble antecedents, who early entered her service as guardian and tutor of her daughter Nefrure. From this relatively modest post he advanced to a position of unprecedented power. In the words of William C. Hayes (*The Scepter of Egypt*, II, 106–107), he added "one important office to another until he had become, in his own words, 'the greatest of the great in the entire land.' The holder of more than eighty titles, chiefly in the administration of the vast properties of the royal family and of the state god Amun . . . in his capacity as High Steward [he] probably controlled in the names of these two great powers a large part of the total resources of the Egyptian Empire. . . . As confident of the female pharaoh and guardian of her daughter he was evidently permitted to conduct himself as if he were a member of the family, enjoying privileges and prerogatives never before accorded to a mere official. . . . His power, however, did not long survive the death of his royal ward Nefrure, and by the nineteenth year of the reign his downfall was complete, his great new tomb at Deir el Bahri abandoned unfinished, and many of his monuments defaced or smashed to pieces."

Had he so far overreached himself that he had designs upon the throne, to be legitimized, perhaps, by marriage to the Queen herself, or was his downfall due to the jealous intrigues of his colleagues, in which Thutmose III had a hand? History gives no answer to that question. Certain it is, however, that Thutmose III, who turned out to be one of the ablest and most energetic kings Egypt ever had, could hardly have been kept so long in subjugation by the Queen had she not been supported by a powerful and ambitious cabal, in which Senenmut held a prominent position.

While Hatshepsut had made for herself two tombs, it is doubtful that she was ever buried in either one of them. It is possible that she met a violent death and was consigned by Thutmose III to an obscure grave in one of the remote wadis of the necropolis. Certain it is that he rescued his revered grandfather, Thutmose I, from the Queen's tomb (to which she had removed his body, as if to continue even after her own death the legend that she had received the crown from his hands) and returned his mummy to rest in the tomb that Ineni had made for him in the Valley of the Kings.

Future generations no longer recognized Hatshepsut as ever having reigned. From the lists of royal ancestors made by subsequent kings her name is omitted, along with those of the heretic Akhenaten and a few other shady rulers who seemed better forgotten.

CHAPTER TWO

The Capital of an Empire

ONCE THUTMOSE III was rid of his hated stepmother and the courtiers who had supported her ambitions he emerged as one of the most remarkable rulers in history. Although we know nothing of how he spent his twenty-one years of subjugation to the Queen, it soon became evident that those years had not been wasted. He immediately turned his face to the East, where revolts in Palestine and Syria threatened the hard-won gains of his forefathers. It took, in all, nineteen years and seventeen arduous campaigns before all the territory on the hither side of the Euphrates, from Asia Minor in the north to the southern boundaries of Palestine, lay under his footstool. His exploits aroused the respect, if not the fear, of nations more powerful than the petty chieftains he had conquered. Princes of Mitanni, who threatened Syria from beyond the Euphrates, paid him tribute; the far-off king of Babylon sent him gifts enriched with lapis lazuli; and emissaries of the Hittites brought to him from their mountain fastnesses of Anatolia heavy rings of silver and other rare and precious offerings.

By the time there was peace in the empire, Thutmose was an old man. For many years his summers had been spent in arduous campaigning. His winters in Egypt brought him no rest. His first care was to make a tour of the land to inspect his multifarious building projects and to see that his subordinates were conscientious in the performance of their duties, without undue oppression of the people. "His Majesty," recorded one of his followers, "was one who knew what happened."

Into the treasuries of king and gods poured tribute and booty in the form of rich equipment and clothing, grain and cattle and captive slaves. Thebes began to be a cosmopolitan city, a babel of strange tongues. Foreign words crept into the language, there were alien slaves in the palaces and temples and in the fields, foreign princesses in the royal harem. The sons of Eastern princes were established in colonies attached to the temples to be taught the Egyptian way of life and to return, well indoctrinated, to inherit the petty kingdoms of Palestine and Syria. For Palestine and Syria were never colonies in the modern sense of the word. There were Egyptian "advisers", in the major cities and Egyptian garrisons at strategic points, but there seems little doubt that Egypt's eastern empire was "God's Land"—the Land of the Pharaoh—only in the loosest sense of the words. The small kingdoms of which the Empire was composed were loyal through greed and fear—greed, because amicable relations with wealthy Egypt were advantageous, fear, not only of Egypt, but of more ruthless enemies who might, and ultimately did, press in from the north and the east, but were temporarily restrained by Egypt's power.

A great part of the wealth that poured into Egypt as a result of Thutmose's conquests was lavished on the temple of Amun at Karnak, which received, among other treasure, annual tribute from certain conquered cities. Thutmose III enlarged the entire precinct and enclosed it in a new wall. One of his first concerns was to wall in, roof high, the two great obelisks of Hatshepsut, in the erecting of which she had partly demolished the hall built by her father. It would have been awkward to remove them, but the King made sure that they were no longer visible from within the temple. He reconstructed the interior of the god's house and made many additions to it. At the main entrance he erected a new pylon and set up a pair of obelisks of his own in front of those of Thutmose I. Behind the Twelfth Dynasty sanctuary, he built for his jubilee a festival hall representing a pavilion in stone with stone columns that imitated wooden tent poles. Near it are to be seen today the remains of a delightful chamber, on the walls of which are depicted with considerable fantasy strange plants and animals which the Pharaoh brought back from his campaigns in Syria.

All this and more Thutmose III built in the temple of Amun. The reliefs and sculptures that he left there show the grace and perfection of finish already apparent in the works of Hatshepsut; and what survives of the buildings and halls which he added to the temple, however overshadowed by the grandiose construction of Ramesses the Great, echoes the dignity and restraint characteristic of the architecture of the earlier New Kingdom. Hardly a trace remains of the temple he dedicated to Hathor near Deir el Bahri; only the beautifully sculptured shrine that once stood in it, showing the King drawing life-giving milk from the Hathor-cow, is preserved in the Cairo Museum. Scarcely more is left of his mortuary temple near the Ramesseum, and his work at Medinet Habu is eclipsed by the additions of the Twentieth Dynasty.

At Karnak and elsewhere he left a written account of his deeds and constructions. Of all the ancient pharaohs, none passed on records of greater historical importance. To establish his royal ancestry, he outlined his lineage on the walls of the temple of Amun, tracing his descent back to the beginning of the Eleventh Dynasty—and furnishing a valuable king list for future historians. There, too, is preserved the account of his campaigns and of the spoils of war, of the victory festivals he endowed for the pleasure of the god and the Theban populace. He claims that he himself planned and supervised the reorganization of the temple administration made necessary by the increasing wealth of Amun and the elaboration of the cult. Nothing, apparently, escaped his notice. Pictured on the walls of the temple are vessels for the divine service ostensibly designed by the royal hand.

Many of the sanctuaries he built throughout the length and breadth of Egypt survive only in the record he left of them. There is no trace of the temple he erected to Harakhte, god of the sunrise, at Heliopolis nor of the two obelisks he dedicated there to Re. Indeed, of all the obelisks he raised to celebrate his jubilees or other occasions—and he was second only to Ramesses the Great in the matter of obelisks—not one is left standing in Egypt, though a number of them grace cities of the modern world. The pair from Heliopolis are the "Cleopatra's Needles" of New York and London, and two of his Theban obelisks have stood respectively in Constantinople and in Rome for nearly two thousand years.

Some of his Nubian monuments (now soon to be destroyed by the floodwaters resulting from the new High Dam) have survived to attest that his power reached far up the Nile. Unlike Palestine and Syria, Nubia was a true colony, ruled over by the "King's Son of Kush." Thutmose III added his name to that of Thutmose I on the rock near the Fifth Cataract, a witness that he established contact with the tribes of the hinterland; during his reign for the first time unmistakable Negroes were depicted on the walls of Egyptian tombs. The King also brought the fertile oases of the Western Desert into closer control—jars of fine vintages bearing the legend "Wine of the Oases" appeared in Theban storerooms—and he resumed the regeneration of the long-neglected Delta, with its broad pastures and rich alluvial lands and its navigable channels leading to the sea and thence to Asia. It is small wonder that his name echoed down the centuries, never entirely eclipsed even by that of the grandiloquent Ramesses. His throne name, Menkheperre, was a potent one on amuletic scarabs almost to the end of ancient Egyptian history. It is one of the few royal epithets known to modern inhabitants of The City, where it has become practically the trade-mark of the false antiquity.

In his great accomplishment Thutmose III was aided by able and devoted men. The New Kingdom saw many changes in the court and the administration of the country. It is significant that the earlier titles connected with what must have been a burdensome and extremely boring ritual circumscribing the daily life of the pharaoh had by now all but disappeared. Nobles were no longer proudly designated, as they had been in the Old Kingdom, as chiefs of the royal hairdressers or manicurists or perfumers. What few similar titles survived, such as Attendant at the King's Levee or Keeper of the Royal Kilt or of the Royal Diadem, Fan Bearer at the King's Right Hand and Royal Butler, "clean of hands," were more or less honorary marks of prestige and favor without connotation of intimate, personal service. This as well as other scattered bits of information seems to indicate not merely that the pharaoh may have enjoyed that modicum of personal privacy allowed to heads of state in any time or place, but chiefly that the demands of an expanding rule had crowded out much of the essentially meaningless ceremonial centered in the person of the divinely descended king.

Even more important is the fact that noble birth was fast ceasing to be the sole prerequisite for high office. The swelling bureaucracy required ability rather than blood. To be a relative of the king or a hereditary count was no longer assurance of an important—and lucrative—post. To be sure, there had occurred in earlier times instances of influential persons' rising from comparative obscurity; but as the Eighteenth Dynasty approached its height, examples multiplied of men, far from aristocratic in origin, who attained positions of power. An ambitious scribe, a humble priest, the husband or son of a nurse to the royal children or of a former harem lady, and, above all, a soldier who had proved his worth on the battlefield, might aspire to high rank if he were intelligent and trustworthy. There was no question of democracy involved in this; it was simply a matter of expediency. The king was as much as he had ever been an absolute monarch, the "Good God" who held the country and its people in his hand.

A number of the followers of Thutmose III have left a record of their services and their devotion in the tombs they built in the Theban necropolis—tombs of a sumptuousness that bears witness to the King's largesse. Chief among them was the vizier of Upper Egypt, Rekhmire, whose name is almost as well known to posterity as that of his royal master. His investiture by the King, who instructed him in the duties of his "bitter" office in what was probably a traditional ceremony, and his excellence in performing those duties are exhaustively recorded on the walls of his Theban tomb.

Of necessity, with the Pharaoh so frequently absent on campaigns in foreign lands and so occupied between times with preparations for the next season's military excursions, the vizier was more than ever before an important person. The office he held was roughly equivalent to that of a modern prime minister, but in addition, he functioned as secretary of war, of the interior, and of agriculture and kept an eye on the treasury. He was, moreover, chief justice and chief of police for Upper Egypt, and also mayor of Thebes. As grand steward of the King and of the temple of Amun, he exercised control over the wealth of a land that was, in essence, simply the joint estate of the King and the god: what property belonged to lesser persons was only held in fief.

Rekhmire tells us that he sat daily in his hall to hear cases and make decisions. He boasts that he never leaned "to one side more than to another side" and that he never accepted a bribe. A little-publicized fragmentary scene in his tomb, however, seems to indicate that, impeccable as the conduct of the Vizier may have been, the hands of his subordinates were perhaps not equally clean. This scene pictures petitioners at the entrance to the hall of Rekhmire. Some grovel in the dust; others surge forward, only to be pushed back by policemen armed with threatening clubs. Some of the suppliants come bearing lengths of cloth, necklaces, jars of unknown content. Are these things to be offered as evidence—or as bribes? Not, perhaps, bribes for the great man himself, but for the attendants upon whom a humble petitioner must depend to gain a hearing. In the light of what we know of

Egypt in more recent times, we can well imagine the court of Rekhmire, the noise, the wailing and recrimination, the crowding and shoving, the undying hope that a gift in the right place may bring, if not justice, at least a hearing—perhaps even the dropping of charges.

While Rekhmire undoubtedly delegated a great part of his duties, one wonders how the days were long enough for him to have accomplished even a modest portion of the work he claims to have done. He was vizier, it is true, only for Upper Egypt, south of Assiut. A second vizier functioned in Lower Egypt, and the powerful viceroy of Kush exercised control over Nubia and the territory south of el Kab. What relationship these men bore to the vizier of the South is unknown, but they must have worked in the closest cooperation with this noble who could boast that he was "second only to the King."

It is also not certain whether the vizier of the North resided at Heliopolis or at Memphis. Heliopolis was a city of hoary antiquity, its foundation buried in the dust of prehistory. It was the seat of the sun-god Re, whose temple, next to that of Amun-Re of Thebes, who had usurped his name and many of his characteristics, was the richest of all Egypt. To the end of the pharaonic period, Heliopolis remained a holy city, a center of religion and learning, which exerted a profound influence on successive generations. It was to Heliopolis that Greek travelers resorted in the hope of learning the secret wisdom jealously guarded by a dwindling priesthood.

Memphis, on the other hand, was politically and economically a more important place. Since its foundation it had been a powerful symbol of United Egypt and of the divine kingship. Menes, the first ruler of the entire country, built his white-walled palace there, and the Temple of Ptah nearby became the traditional scene of coronation, where the pharaohs assumed the Double Crown. There, too, originated the *sed* festival, the jubilee of the ruler, during which the uniting of the Two Lands and the founding of the first palace were re-enacted and the king's title to the succession reaffirmed.

Unlike Memphis—and indeed most world centers—Thebes possessed few geographical advantages aside from its wide, arable plain and the great beauty of its site. It was not a seaport, not even an important river port. It was protected by no natural fortification. It neither commanded a trade route nor defended a border. It was inconveniently situated for the control of Lower Egypt and the land and sea routes to Asia. Herodotos tells us that, in his time, Thebes was nine days' journey from Heliopolis (the latter, around fourteen miles from Memphis as the bird flies). It required at least half again as long to reach The City from the sea. While special couriers may have been able to reduce this time, it may readily be seen that the location of Thebes was not of the handiest, either for internal administration or for world conquest.

Standing as it did near the apex of the Delta, Memphis was at the very juncture of the Two Lands. In the Eighteenth Dynasty it served as a second capital, less rich than Thebes, but rivaling it in importance. It was there that troops gathered, that fleets were built, that commissaries were established for the conquest of Asia. It was there that trading vessels unloaded the products of foreign lands and took on cargoes for the East. Great warehouses and granaries arose there; even Amun of Thebes had his entrepôts at the ancient capital. Kings and princes built palaces and peopled them with harem ladies on an elevation overlooking the temples and groves and the huge artificial lake that had been made at the command of rulers of the Old Kingdom. The pharaohs of the Eighteenth Dynasty, devoted as they were to Amun, saw to it that the sanctuaries of the old Memphite gods were not neglected. Among those ancient shrines arose new temples dedicated to strange Syrian deities, for even more than Thebes, Memphis was a cosmopolitan city, colorful with foreign visitors and traders, immigrants and slaves and hostages, and so it remained. Strabo reported that it was inhabited, like Alexandria, with "mixed races of people."

Today hardly more than a few scattered stones tell where Memphis once stood. The mud brick of which houses and magazines and palaces were built has crumbled to dust. The temples have long since been sacked, their stones carried off for use in the mosques and fortifications of medieval Cairo. Among the palm groves and fields that cover the site lies a colossus of Ramesses the Great, which once stood before the Temple of Ptah; here and there crops up a fragment of sculptured stone or the trace of an ancient foundation. Only the pyramids and the vast cemeteries at the desert's edge remain as witnesses to the long history of a once great and populous city.

Thutmose III must of necessity have spent much time in the ancient capital in preparation for his campaigns in Asia. Some scholars suspect that he visited Thebes only for the Feast of Opet, that greatest of Theban festivals. His successors, when not actually born in one of the royal palaces at Memphis, certainly received their early education in the region.

The education of princes probably included instruction in reading and writing and in at least the forms of religious ceremonial; but in the age of conquest and expansion, the emphasis seems to have been chiefly on the so-called manly virtues. Amunhotep II, the son and heir of the Conqueror, has left a picturesque record of his youthful training on a stela he set up in a now-vanished sanctuary which he built to the god Harmachis in the neighborhood of the Great Sphinx because he "remembered the place where he had enjoyed himself in his youth." According to his statement, he excelled from an early age in all the arts of the old Theban war god Montu, surpassing all others in drawing his great bow. He was, moreover—to the joy of the Syrian divinities, Reshep and Astarte—so skilled in the handling of horses that his father put him in charge of the royal Memphite stables while he was still little more than a boy; and he was not yet eighteen when his skill and endurance on the water won him the command of the chief base and dockyard of the Egyptian Navy at Peru-nefer—a name that Dr. Hayes suggests may have signified something like *Bon Voyage!*

Once his father had gone to join the gods, Amunhotep II had occasion to test his prowess, for the princelings of the East combined to put all of Syria north of the Palestinian border into turmoil. He quelled the uprising in a single campaign and brought back to Thebes the bodies of seven of the ring-leaders. Six he hung head down on the walls of the Temple of Amun for all to see, and the seventh was carried to far-off Napata near the Fourth Cataract to be exhibited as a grisly reminder to Nubian chieftains of what could happen to those who opposed the might of a pharaoh. Barbarous, yes. But it is not so very long since the heads of traitors rotted impaled at the Tower of London; almost within memory the lifeless bodies of malefactors were left to clank a dismal warning from the gallows on Tyburn Hill; and our fathers can tell us of times when executions throughout the "civilized" world furnished occasion for ghoulish holidays. As for the unspeakable atrocities of our own generation—they have unhappily become all but commonplace.

Amunhotep's cruel object lesson was not completely effective, for two more expeditions seem to have taken place before the East was subdued. After that we hear no more of revolts in Syria or Nubia during his reign of twenty-six years. Tribute and especially trade now took the place of booty to fill the treasuries of king and gods. Even more important than what came from the Syrian provinces were the products of pacified Nubia, the "Gold Country of Amun." That region not only supplied soldiers and many slaves, ebony and other precious woods from the equatorial forests, skins of animals for royal and priestly regalia, ostrich feathers for the great flabella used in the pageantry of gods and kings, but also, and above all, gold. Egypt possessed other sources of the precious metal— the mines of the Eastern Desert, exploited from time immemorial, still yielded—but the richest of all were the mountains to the east of Nubia. In torrid, desolate country, many days' travel south of the border, remains still exist of wretched, waterless villages where captives and exiled criminals lived and died mining gold for the enrichment of Egypt.

During the New Kingdom the annual revenue from Nubian mines reached staggering figures. Gold was the principal item of trade with foreign countries. It was used, too, as in modern times, for subsidies—"gifts"—to Eastern potentates, in the hope that they might keep the peace or lend their support to the right side. Fashioned into rings or ingots of various standard weights, gold served, along with silver and copper, in the place of coinage, though the actual metal entered into only a limited number of transactions, and barter in kind remained the common method of exchange. While commodities might be worth a given weight of copper or silver or gold, they were often valued in such things as measures of grain; and frequently goods were simply swapped without reference to any standard save the mutual need of the parties to the trade.

Apart from its rarity and value gold was prized, as it has ever been, for its beauty. It was coveted for its gleam, rivaling that of the sun. It was, moreover, "everlasting," subject to neither rust nor decay, and thus it acquired a mystic, symbolic value beyond its intrinsic worth: it was the very substance of the eternal gods. Deserving servants of the pharaoh might receive the "gold of valor" at his hands, but this finest of metals was largely reserved for royalty and divinity. Deified monarchs went to their last rest in coffins of gold. The shrines and statues of the gods and the approaches to their sanctuaries blazed with gold, and golden vessels crowded the storerooms of temples. Pillars, portals, and relief-covered walls still show the marks of gold sheathing, long ago torn off by plunderers who did not fear divine wrath.

Amunhotep II, like his predecessors, spent much of his great wealth in building and ornamenting the temples of his kingdom. He added to and improved the temple of Amun, which was fast becoming the vast and confusing complex that time and pillage have never been able to destroy entirely. He completed, in so far as possible, the restoration of the hall of Thutmose I, at the end of which Hatshepsut had set up her obelisks, and built a small temple of his own to the south of the main sanctuary. While there is evidence that he embellished the temple at Karnak still further, not much remains of his work there; and very little is left of the other structures that he erected throughout Egypt. Hardly more than the site of the funerary temple he built near that of his father in the Theban necropolis is now distinguishable, though records show that it was still functioning some three hundred years after his death. This is a fact worthy of note, for while such memorials were endowed in perpetuity, memories were often short in the Nile Valley, as indeed elsewhere, and structures were frequently demolished and their income diverted to other uses by kings unmindful of their forefathers. The Instructions for King Merikare, written long before Thebes became great—"Harm not the monument of another. . . . Build not thy tomb out of what has been pulled down!"—though it became a copybook maxim for New Kingdom student scribes, too often went unheeded.

The tomb of Amunhotep II, which rivaled that of his illustrious father in size, is still to be seen in the Valley of the Kings. Its walls, like those of the tombs of his royal companions in death, are decorated, rather dryly, in the style of an unrolled papyrus, containing texts and illustrations from funerary works describing the stages of the night journey of the sun god and the dead King through the Underworld. Such works served more or less as guidebooks to Eternity, providing magical texts to be used against the perils encountered along the road to bliss.

It was quite otherwise with the tombs of the King's courtiers. On their walls were depicted scenes of this fair world, the possessions and pleasures and honors that the owners of the tombs had enjoyed in life or hoped might be theirs in the undiscovered country beyond the grave. Among the tombs of persons prominent during the reign of Amunhotep

II are some of the most beautifully decorated of the Theban necropolis. They tell much of the growing wealth of Egypt and the increasing sumptuousness of court life. From burials of his reign come many of the beautiful objects in our museums, including delicate vases of multicolored glass. These are among the first glass vessels of history. They are antedated only by a few very fragmentary jars found in the tombs of Thutmose III and Amunhotep I.

The inscriptions in the tombs of the followers of Amunhotep II give a glimpse of the character of the King, of the gratitude and trust he showed to friends of his youth and to his companions-at-arms. One of the finest burials is that of Kenamun, the son of Amunhotep's nurse and the playmate of his childhood, who bore many titles, the proudest of which was "Foster Brother of the Lord of the Two Lands," though that of "Steward of the Royal Estates" at Memphis was certainly more remunerative. The husband of another royal nurse, Sennefer, became mayor of Thebes, and his brother Amunemopet attained to the vizierate. Instructors of the King's youth also received splendid burials; among them was the archer Miny, who had taught the Pharaoh to draw his strong bow.

Harsh as he may have been toward his enemies, Amunhotep was seemingly always mindful of his friends. Toward the close of his reign, he sent a letter to an officer named Wesersatet, who had shared the hardships and pleasures of his youthful campaign in Syria. This letter, written during a feast following his jubilee, when Amunhotep, mellow with wine, thought of the good old days and his absent companion, is one of the few informal documents we have from a royal hand; and Wesersatet, who had been suitably rewarded with the high office of viceroy of Kush, proudly had it copied in stone at the far-off Fortress of Semna, near the Second Cataract. In his letter the King refers contemptuously to his conquered Syrian enemies as "old women" and warns his one-time companion against the machinations and magic of the Nubians.

Amunhotep's tomb was rifled in antiquity, but the robbers left behind the bow inscribed with his name and the legend "Smiter of the Troglodytes, overthrower of Kush, hacking up their cities . . . the Great Wall of Egypt, protector of his soldiers." They also left his mummy, stripped of treasure but still garlanded with flowers that were fresh some three millennia ago. The poor shriveled remains give small idea of his reputed physical prowess or of the force of character that made him a great ruler. Still less do his sculptures, which show him as a slender, beautiful, and rather empty-faced youth.

Save during the brief eruption of "Amarna art," royal sculptures of the New Kingdom are almost without exception highly idealized. While those of the earlier reigns possess great perfection of finish and a strange, frozen beauty, they are without much individuality. Certain family features such as the "Thutmosid nose" recur again and again, but it is frequently impossible, unless aided by an inscription, to tell one of the Thutmosid succession from another; even sculptures of Hatshepsut and Thutmose III are sometimes indistinguishable. In the reign of Amunhotep II, the formula becomes rather boringly stereotyped; but it is during his rule, nevertheless, that tomb painting and private sculptures show a first vague presage of the revolution in art that was to culminate in the pseudo-realism of the Amarna period.

Of Amunhotep's son and successor, Thutmose IV, we catch only clouded glimpses. He was born of the Great Royal Wife Tia, his father's half-sister, and died as a young man after a very brief reign. He apparently grew up in the Memphite region, campaigned briefly in Syria and Nubia, built a funerary temple near those of his father and grandfather, and initiated the preparation of a tomb in the Valley of the Kings. His tomb was never finished, but excavations in 1904 gleaned from it such remnants of its regal equipment as ancient tomb robbers had scorned. These included a chariot ornamented with reliefs that are extraordinarily free in style and also the earliest examples of textiles with recognizable colored patterns that have survived from Egypt or indeed from anywhere else in the world. Among them are some bearing the names of Thutmose III and Amunhotep II, an indication that they were rarities, treasured as heirlooms. Though their ornament is Egyptian, they were probably inspired from the East; they seem to reflect the Oriental taste for opulence that was gradually transforming the compartive austerity of Egyptian decorative arts.

The story of a youthful dream of Thutmose IV, long preserved in folklore, is told on a stela which he set up between the paws of the Great Sphinx at Giza. There the King relates that one day, as he returned from hunting in the desert in his chariot drawn by horses "swifter than the wind," he stopped to rest in the shadow of the Sphinx. He fell asleep, and the Sphinx spoke to him in a vision.

As we know today, the Sphinx is a royal monument, its head in the likeness of the great King Khafre (Chephren) of the Fourth Dynasty, its body that of an all-powerful lion. But to men of the Eighteenth Dynasty, some thousand years after the colossal figure had been carved out of an outcrop of desert rock, it was a representation of the god Harmachis—"Horus-on-the-Horizon." As the god, therefore, it spoke to the sleeping prince, begging him to clear away the encroaching sand in which it was half-buried, for "Behold, my state is like one who is in pain, and my entire body is out of joint." In return for this service, Harmachis promised the prince the crown of Egypt, the rule of the earth in its length and breadth, the products of the Two Lands and of every foreign country.

A strange promise, and one not made by the state god, Amun-Re, begetter of kings. It gives rise to the suspicion that Thutmose may not have been in the direct line of succession and hints, moreover, that this northern-bred prince (as indeed his father before him) may have been yearning after the solar cult of Heliopolis, from which was to be engendered the heresy that resulted in the temporary eclipse of Amun-Re, the downfall of the dynasty, and the beginning of the long decline of Thebes.

The only other significant fact that emerges from Thutmose IV's brief rule is that of his alliance with a daughter of the King of Mitanni, alternatingly the enemy and the capricious ally of the Theban house. This was not the first time that kings of Egypt had taken to wife princesses of foreign origin, nor was it to be the last. Thutmose III had in his well-peopled harem three wives with foreign names, who were presumably daughters of Eastern rulers. They were buried in a single tomb, hidden in a remote wadi not far from the Valley of the Kings, which has yielded rich treasure worthy of their rank. We do not know whether these princesses were brought to Egypt as captives or came as the result of diplomatic alliance. But it is certain that the marriage of Thutmose IV to the Mitannian princess was the product of long negotiation with her royal father and marked the beginning of a trend toward maintaining peace with the East through "traditional diplomatic channels."

Some have thought that this princess, whose name is not known, became the Great Royal Wife of Thutmose IV under the Egyptian name of Mutemwiya. However that may be, it was Mutemwiya who bore the last of the great rulers of the Eighteenth Dynasty, Amunhotep III, the Magnificent.

CHAPTER THREE

The City in Its Prime

THE THEBES to which Amunhotep III fell heir was a city of contrasts, of hardly conceivable splendor, and of squalor. It could boast one of the most beautiful sites in all Egypt. There the Nile on its way to the sea, after long confinement between rocky banks, broadened into a wide, island-studded expanse. On the west rose the forbidding cliffs of the desert plateau, broken by deep, twisting wadis and descending in a series of rugged, irregular terraces to a ribbon of cultivated land. On the east the tawny desert hills receded, leaving a broad, well-watered plain dotted with groves.

On both sides of the river the scene was dominated by temples, vaster and more numerous and more brilliant than can be imagined from what remains of them today. At the foot of the western cliffs stretched a line of funerary sanctuaries built by Amunhotep's ancestors, surrounded by groves and gardens and approached from the Nile by gleaming canals or broad ways. Around their encircling walls clustered villages, and the cliffs above them were honeycombed with the porticoed tombs of great Thebans. On the eastern bank was The City proper, lying behind and around the great temple of Amun and his Southern Sanctuary, both at the water's edge.

The very humble could never hope to penetrate the awful interiors of the temples of the gods and the deified kings, but they could see, rising above the enclosure walls, the brightly painted cornices of the pylons, the tall, electrum-tipped flag-staves fluttering gay pennants into the sky and the summits of giant obelisks crowned with gold-sheathed pyramidions that mimicked the rays of the sun. On feast days the little people could watch the great god, housed in a jeweled shrine, as he was carried in a litter by white-robed priests along a wide, sphinx-lined avenue or sailed the broad Nile in his gleaming bark. They might even, before they prostrated themselves in the dust, see the King, no less gorgeous than the god, as he issued from temple or palace precinct.

Inland from the Nile, eastern Thebes was a city of narrow, meandering streets lined with blank walls broken by low doors or more pretentious portals. Such few windows as faced the street were set high, beyond the reach of prying eyes or pilfering hands. Here and there an open door showed a craftsman at work or offered a fleeting vision of a garden, rich with shade and sweet-scented flowers—a welcome rest for eyes dazzled by the pitiless glare of Upper Egyptian days and dimmed by dust and clinging, persistent flies.

Dust and flies there were in abundance, and smells that overpowered the fragrance of flowers and incense. The dust from incessant razing and building, from busy, unpaved streets and lanes filled the air with a thin haze. As for flies, they were a plague of Egypt long before the time of Moses. In the little world of the tomb-paintings, even the King's Great Wife is depicted with a fly whisk not unlike those offered to the tourist in Karnak village today. Ancient Thebes was infested with other vermin of which the tomb paintings give no hint. There were gnats and fleas and lice, scorpions and deadly snakes; from time to time locusts stripped the fields; rats and mice haunted the storerooms.

The smell of Thebes must have been similar to the mixed, not altogether unpleasant odor of an Oriental town of the present day, a smell of hot dust and pungent, aromatic burning dung and charcoal, the stench of fish and meat drying on flat roofs, a pervasive reek of ammonia. While the houses of the rich were provided with bathrooms and latrines, there was no real sanitation. Waste water drained into the subsoil. Refuse was dumped wherever handy, to be disposed of by scavenging birds and dogs and jackals and purified by the sun. Byres for cattle frequently adjoined the villas of the well-to-do, and animals were tethered in the meager courtyards of hovels or shared cramped rooms with their owners. There were no conveniences in the houses of the poor.

Thebes had been a city of gradual, haphazard growth. Homer to the contrary, it was apparently never enclosed within walls; his often quoted reference to its "hundred gates" was inspired (as the not always perspicacious Diodorus guessed in the first century before our era) by the many pylons of its temples. The city sprawled, ungirded, along the Nile, swallowing country houses and hamlets as it grew, here surrounding, there demolishing and rebuilding. It had its fine villas, enclosed in gardens, its tall, mud brick town houses, similar to the gaunt adobe dwellings of three stories or more that today cluster in Arabian towns; it had its government buildings and magazines, its busy quais, its palaces, and its few wide processional ways. But slums edged into its grandeur. Workshops and mean dwellings were neighbors of the great, and on market days crazy booths made of palm branches crouched against temple and palace walls.

Thebes was a noisy city. The quais were loud with the shouts and songs of workers who unloaded the boats bringing

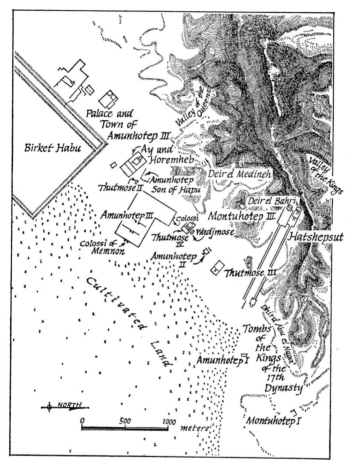

Birket Habu

Palace and Town of Amunhotep III

Valley of the Queens

Ay and Horemheb

Amunhotep Son of Hapu

Thutmose II

Deir el Medineh

Valley of the Kings

Amunhotep III

Colossi

Deir el Bahri

Montuhotep III

Wadjmose

Hatshepsut

Thutmose IV

Colossi of Memnon

Amunhotep II

Thutmose III

Dra'a Abu el Naga

Cultivated Land

Tombs of the Kings of the 17th Dynasty

Amunhotep I

NORTH

0   500   1000   meters

Montuhotep I

Plan of the West Bank of Thebes

Adapted from Hölscher's *The Temples of the Eighteenth Dynasty* from all of Egypt and the far reaches of the empire produce and precious wares for the treasuries of gods and king and fine stone for temples and sculptures. The streets echoed with the cries of donkey boys and porters. Workmen hoisted great blocks into place to a chanted rhythm. Slaves making bricks out of Nile mud chattered in alien tongues and crooned strange songs as they worked. Over all rose the staccato commands of overseers and the cracking of whips. In the narrow streets the hammer and clank of craftsmen at work mingled with the shrill voices of women and the shouts and wails of naked children.

From dawn to dusk the noise never ceased. But after sunset, the clamor died away. Few were abroad by night. The stillness was broken only by the barking and howling of dogs and jackals and the occasional anguished protest of a donkey. Perhaps on evenings of full moon, there rose from the Nile, as sometimes today, haunting, ancient melodies, sung from skiff to skiff in monotonous antiphony, to the syncopated accompaniment of drums. So, at least, it may be imagined.

Actually, we know very little of The City in its prime. Its extent, its topography, its physical aspect are all lost. Except for the remnants of temples built of enduring stone, there is almost nothing left of the onetime capital of the world. Hovels and palaces alike were constructed of sun-dried brick and have long since vanished. Only rarely have archaeologists stumbled on the poor foundations of ancient dwellings from which to hazard a guess about the structures once raised on them. From their findings in the neighborhood of Thebes and elsewhere in Egypt, from tantalizingly incomplete and often enigmatic written records, from scenes on the walls of tombs, from modern analogies in the slow-changing pattern of the East, we have to put together the picture of Thebes, its people and their lives. What we have is a gigantic jigsaw puzzle, from which many pieces have been lost.

Prior to the Eighteenth Dynasty, there were perhaps few centers in argicultural Egypt that could properly be called cities, and it is difficult to determine how nearly any of the cities called into being by the prosperity of the Empire approximated to the modern meaning of the word. Most of them lie buried deep under successive layers of habitation; only their names sometimes survive in quaint distortion. Many others have been carried off piecemeal, the stones of their temples used by generations of builders and the disintegrated mud brick and refuse of their houses by generations of peasants, for there is no fertilizer as good or as cheap as the nitrogen-rich detritus of antiquity. Only one great city has left traces unobscured by subsequent settlement—the city known today as Amarna, the capital founded by Akhenaten, the son and successor of Amunhotep III, some two hundred and fifty miles down-river from Thebes. Built almost over night and completely abandoned before it was a quarter-century old, it is hardly typical of a center of gradual growth such as Thebes but yet presents many features that must have been common to The City in its prime.

Partially razed in antiquity and subject to more than three thousand years of weathering and depredation, it owes such preservation as it has to its isolation. The site chosen by Akhenaten for his capital was a desolate one, a bay in the Eastern Desert, with encircling cliffs that curved on the north and the south to the edge of the Nile. A very narrow strip of cultivable land fringed the river, but on the opposite shore the desert receded, leaving a watered plain to supply the city with produce. In the barren bay the capital called Akhetaten, "Horizon-of-the-Aten," was laid out on virgin soil with what seems to have been, under the circumstances, a remarkable lack of systematic planning.

A wide highway nearly eight miles long, dubbed by archaeologists the "Royal Road," followed the course of the river. Inland and roughly parallel with it were two narrower roads, and at irregular intervals these three main arteries were intersected by streets and lanes at more or less right angles to them, but frequently twisting into *culs-de-sac*. Along these ways the city sprang up at random. Only the central section, containing the great temple and the royal palaces, seems to have been constructed with foresight. There the Royal Road widened to an impressive two hundred and fifty yards. On the west lay the official palace, where the King held court. This was connected with the Royal Residence on the opposite side of the road by a covered bridge approached by ramps and bearing in its center a small room with a balcony, the "Window of Appearances," where the Pharaoh showed himself from time to time to reward the faithful with gifts of gold and to receive the adulation of the multitude. Adjacent to the walled enclosure of the Residence, the largest secular building of antiquity, which contained the King's apartments, a private chapel, clustering dependencies, and an extensive garden, was the Great Temple of the Aten with its sun-drenched sanctuary, so unlike the dim holy of holies where Amun dwelt, but similar to the ancient sun temples of the north. It was perhaps the greatest temple ever built in a single reign. Its walls had a frontage of a thousand feet and reached more than twenty-five hundred feet back into the desert.

Completed toward the end of Akhenaten's brief, seventeen-year rule, it included within its precincts earlier, hastily built shrines of mud brick.

Behind this vast complex of royal and divine habitation were strewn in a rather haphazard fashion the public buildings—archives, scriptorium, administrative offices, houses for temple and government personnel—and bordering these to the east were military barracks and long rows of stables. Beyond lay the desert, empty save for random altars and, in a hollow invisible from the city, a walled, carefully guarded village where lived workmen engaged in building and decorating tombs in the barren cliffs.

Along the Royal Road and scattered here and there on subsidiary ways were villas. These houses, built as they were on unencumbered soil, were probably larger and set in more ample grounds than Theban villas, but to judge from representations in tombs and from other evidence, they followed much the same plan. They were almost square and usually of a single story. Some contained as many as thirty or forty rooms. A central, pillared hall, higher than the surrounding rooms to allow for clerestory lighting, was approached on one side by an anteroom and an ample loggia. On the other three sides clustered smaller halls, quarters for guests and for the women of the family, and a suite of bedroom, bathroom, and latrine for the master. On the roof, approached by a staircase, was a pavilion oriented to the cool north breeze. The rooms were whitewashed and decorated with gay floral friezes. Painted pillars, cushioned chairs and divans, and mats of tinted grasses lent an airy luxury.

Each house was contained in a walled enclosure, which embraced also a kitchen, servants' quarters, stables, storerooms, and huge domed granaries. In crowded Thebes, such granaries, as well as ovens for baking bread, were sometimes on the roofs of houses. Every enclosure at Amarna contained a garden, often with a pool and a small chapel in its midst, for a garden was a necessary adjunct to any fine Egyptian house, to any palace or temple. Some of those represented on the walls of Theban tombs contain specimens of nearly all the trees grown in Egypt, and their pictured pools are stocked with fish and fringed with lotus. At Amarna the rocky, alkaline soil presented special problems for the gardener. Trees and flowers had to be planted in pits filled with rich earth brought from the riverside and deep wells had to be sunk to reach seeping ground water to supply the gardens and their owners.

Akhetaten had no tall houses such as are known to have been erected in more populous Thebes, but otherwise the city showed the same lack of zoning or of studied plan as must have existed to a more marked degree in the old capital. Pretentious dwellings alternated with workshops and modest houses, and especially in the northern section of the city, slums edged into quarters of comfortable bourgeois homes. There were neither sewers nor gutters to carry off waste; dumps littered the open spaces, even in the shadow of palace walls; the great Royal Road itself was never paved, only leveled and scraped.

Akhetaten has long since returned to the desert, which has left only skeleton traces of its hasty grandeur. In its day, the ephemeral capital must have been almost as busy and noisy as Thebes. It must have been filled with the dust and clamor of construction, which never ceased so long as the city lasted; and the Nile that flowed past it, now all but empty, must have seen the coming and going of many ships loaded with supplies and building materials. Some of the ships brought foreign envoys who came to sue in vain the support and favor of a king lost in contemplation of himself and his god.

Isolated as it was and alienated from a tradition-bound people by a ruler who sought to destroy tradition, Akhetaten could never have been the living heart of the land that Thebes was; but, nevertheless, this later, short-lived city can help fill out the picture of what the older capital may once have been. Thebes was probably never more beautiful than it was during the rule of Amunhotep III. Although after the Amarna interlude, successive kings continued to pour wealth into The City, to add to its ancient temples and to build new ones, their constructions never equaled those of the Eighteenth Dynasty in taste and elegance; and of all the builders of that dynasty, Amunhotep III was the greatest.

Although many of his works have vanished, the beautiful temple of Luxor, the Southern Harem of Amun, still stands as a monument to him. It has suffered many vicissitudes. A Roman garrison was once quartered in its halls, leaving remains of mud brick barracks to be buried under gradually accumulating debris. Later, part of it served as a Christian church. With the coming of the Arabs, it gave a name— Luxor, a corruption of "el Aksur," "the Castles"—to the modern town that had grown in and around it. Within a generation or two of our own time, houses of Luxor families clung like birds' nests under its architraves; and an ancient mosque still perches on a mound of debris in one corner of it —a mosque whose Islamic saint makes an annual journey through the streets in a boat, echoing the voyages of Amun in his splendid bark borne on the shoulders of priests of a forgotten faith. Now, mostly freed from the detritus of ages, the vast temple, roofless as it is, shows clearly what an Eighteenth Dynasty temple must have been.

It was conceived as a palace with courts and pillared halls leading to intimate apartments, where the deity could live and take his pleasure. It was god's house, in the most literal sense of the words; and in one of the inner chambers, Amunhotep III had his miraculous birth as the son of Amun-Re depicted, as Hatshepsut had recorded a similar wonder on the walls of her temple at Deir el Bahri. The central colonnade of the temple, as might be expected from so magnificent a king, is higher and larger than any built under former rulers; but the columns composing it, although fifty-two feet tall, are so spaced and proportioned that their immensity is neither heavy nor oppressive.

For the convenience of the god, Amunhotep constructed a broad way leading from the temple of Karnak to that of Luxor. This mile-long road was flanked by rows of couchant rams, avatars of Amun, each with a figure of the King standing between its forelegs; some of them still remain to be climbed upon by the swarming children of Karnak village. A branch road, also lined with criosphinxes, led from this processional way to the temple the Pharaoh built for the goddess Mut, the consort of Amun. Among the ruins of her temple are some of the scores of over-life-size figures of the lion-headed Sekhmet with which he once adorned it, for as a consequence of the Theban ambition to make Amun "the universal lord, beginning of existing things" and chief of all the gods, Sekhmet, the wife of the Memphite Ptah, had come to be identified with Mut. So numerous were these sculptures of black basalt that there is hardly a museum of any consequence in the Western world that does not possess one or a fragment of one.

In far-distant Nubia, Amunhotep built the finest temple of that subject land at Sulb, north of the Third Cataract. Still impressive in ruin, this temple once rivaled that of Luxor in beauty and may indeed have been planned by the same architect. It, too, had its avenue of rams; and it contained a magnificent granite sculpture representing the King as a lion, which is now in the British Museum. At Sulb and also at Memphis, where he dedicated a shrine to himself and the god Ptah, Amunhotep initiated the worship of his own "living image," and he erected a temple near Sulb for the cult of his Queen.

The King, of course, did not neglect the temple of Amun at Karnak. There he constructed the great pylon, for which he demolished the lovely chapel of Senwosret I. On the front of the gateway was "the Divine Shadow as a ram, inlaid with real lapis lazuli and wrought with gold and many costly stones," and on the back of the pylon were recorded the rich gifts which the Pharaoh had made to his father, the god. At the northern entrance to the temple enclosure, he erected a chapel to Amun, which was, in the King's own words, "a marvelous thing . . . plentiful in gold, unlimited in malachite and lapis lazuli, a place of rest for the Lord of Gods, made like his throne that is in heaven" and set in "an enclosure made to shine with all flowers." A gigantic stone scarab which Amunhotep raised up in honor of the sun god Atum-Kheper-Re still stands on its high plinth overlooking the Sacred Lake of Karnak. Beyond it, at the beginning of the road linking Karnak with the temple of Mut, he erected two colossal figures of himself. On the base of one of them, the King's architect, Amunhotep, son of Hapu, records, "I established the statue in this great temple that it might endure as long as the heavens. You are my witnesses, you who shall come later." Alas, for us who come later, only the foot and ankle of one of the pair remains, though that fragment reaches to the height of a man's waist.

More is left of two other gigantic sculptures of the King, the so-called colossi of Memnon, which stood before his funerary temple on the West Bank. That vast temple, sumptuous beyond all its predecessors, has disappeared, leaving scarcely a trace; but the battered colossi rise out of the green fields of modern cultivation, gaining in grandeur through their isolation. Quartzite monoliths, now lacking their high crowns, they were once nearly seventy feet in height; their middle fingers are four and one-half feet long. They were quarried in the "Red Mountain," far down the river near Memphis, and cut under the supervision of the same Amunhotep who directed the making of the Karnak colossi and other of the King's works, probably the temple of Luxor itself. This architect, who claimed to be "the two eyes of the King of Lower Egypt, the two ears of the King of Upper Egypt," never attained to any of the highest offices of the land, but he gained such favor with the Pharaoh that he was awarded the unique boon of a funerary temple of his own not far from that of the royal master he served so well. Ironically enough, Amunhotep's eponymous architect was revered as a sage and worshiped as a demigod in the Graeco-Roman period, when few remembered whom the great colossi portrayed. The Greeks and Romans thought them to be images of Memnon, a Greek hero who had fallen at Troy.

Not far from his funerary temple in West-of-the-City, Amunhotep III built his chief residence. It is not known why he chose a site in the necropolis. No remains of palaces of former kings have been discovered there. There is reason to believe that certain earlier rulers may have had on the West Bank what amounted to *pieds-à-terre*, similar to the surviving construction of Ramesses III at Medinet Habu, which was little more than a sumptuous rest house to which the Pharaoh could retire with his retinue when he came to celebrate the festivals held in the necropolis. Amunhotep III had other palaces, one at Memphis, one at the entrance to the Fayum, probably one in Eastern Thebes, and almost certainly minor dwellings elsewhere, but the palace on the West Bank was the center from which he ruled. He may have chosen the site simply because it offered ample space for grandiose construction. Though a modern scholar had suggested that he sought a retreat remote from Amun and his priesthood, the emplacement was hardly remote even in days of slow travel; and the King, though he paid respect to the emerging Aten, had no quarrel with his dynastic god, still less with the priests of Karnak, who were his creatures.

It is possible that by the time of Amunhotep III, the necropolis had become rather more the center of things and even more populous than the Thebes clustered around the temples of Karnak and Luxor. While we know nothing of how the population of the sprawling city was distributed, the West Bank must have been a busy place, swarming with officiants and servants and slaves dedicated to the temples of departed kings and with hundreds of laborers and craftsmen working in the service of the dead. The men engaged in building and decorating the royal temples and the ever more splendid private tombs, the sculptors who "gave birth" to the statues of gods and kings and notables, the sarcophagus makers, the embalmers, the omnipresent scribes attached to every department of work—all these and their families lived in hamlets scattered through the necropolis, as did the butchers and bakers and weavers who supplied the needs of living and dead. Villages of peasants fringed the fields; other villages housed the police force. It is thought that the vizier had his office on the West Bank, and other high officials doubtless found it convenient to live near the royal residence, in addition to those closest to the King, who had houses provided for them within the *enceinte* of his palace.

That palace was a long time abuilding. Its construction covered about three-quarters of the Pharaoh's thirty-eight-year reign, and by the time Amunhotep went to his eternal home, it had spread over some eighty acres. Its ruins have been known to archaeologists and subject to haphazard excavation for the greater part of a century and for as long or longer to the local peasantry, who eloquently dubbed the site "Malkata"—"Place-Where-Things-Are-Picked-Up." Enough remained, however, for scientific excavation by an American institution, the Metropolitan Museum of Art, to recover the general plan of the palace, something of its history, and much of the detail of its construction and ornamentation.

It was a city in miniature, rather than a palace. Included within its walls were at least four rambling, one-story dwellings for the King, his two principal wives, and possibly the crown prince. Though the palace was called "Splendor-of-the-Aten" (later, "House of Rejoicing"), a temple within its girdling wall was dedicated to Amun-Re. The *enceinte* also contained administrative buildings, mansions for the chief

dignitaries of the court, smaller houses for lesser officials, servants' quarters, kitchens, storehouses, workshops, and groups
of crowded tenements for the laborers and craftsmen engaged in construction and repair, all built more or less at random around the principal buildings and their wide courts.
A causeway linked the area with the royal funerary temple a
mile away, and a canal led to the highway of the Nile from an
artificial lake that served as a harbor.

The agglomeration of buildings was constructed of sun-
dried brick, plastered inside and out with whitewashed mud.
Little stone was used even in the temple, none in the dwellings save that serving as bases for wooden columns, occasional
doorsills, and bathroom floors. Shoddy as the construction
was, the ensemble was brilliant. The labyrinthine palace in
which the King himself lived had two audience halls, one a
hundred feet long, and a number of smaller halls for more
intimate reception. His private apartments led from a large
columned hall, which had at one end a throne room opening
into royal robing room, bedroom, and bath, and along the
two sides cozy suites for the principal ladies of the harem.

All of these rooms were whitewashed and gaily painted.
On the dais and steps of the throne, symbolically at the feet
of the Pharaoh, were pictured bound Asiatic and Nubian
captives in colorful, outlandish dress; above, elaborate triple
canopies shone with friezes of royal cobra heads and other
devices in colored ceramics and gold. Around the King's
bedroom were painted dancing figures of Bes, that grotesque
and genial household god, with leonine head and bowlegged
dwarf's body, who was worshiped by great and small as
patron of the bedchamber, of dress and cosmetics, of music
and dancing, of the intimate pleasures of domesticity. The

decoration of the great hall reflected the Egyptian love of nature, more than ever apparent during Amunhotep's time and that of his son. The floor was painted to represent a rush-bordered lake populated with fish and waterfowl, and birds winged their way across the sky-blue ceiling. The ceiling of another room mimicked a grape arbor, and on the walls of still another was pictured a desert scene with shy animals among sparse herbage. Ceramic decorations of purple grape clusters, lotus flowers and daisies, birds and fish, and amuletic signs signifying long life and health and power added glitter to door and window frames inside and outside the palace; and over and over again, the King's throne name, Nebmaatre, "Lord-of-Truth-Is-Re," was written in letters of gold.

Some of the decoration was carelessly executed, and much of it, before the colors had softened and the gold leaf had been stripped off, must have been garish. But it showed the gaiety and freedom that was to find a final, untrammeled expression at Amarna. This freedom may have been learned in part from the livelier art of the Aegean. From farther east and from barbaric Africa came a less desirable trend toward gaudy ostentation, so foreign to earlier, more austere periods of Egyptian culture. Such ostentation is apparent, not only in the leaning toward the colossal in architecture and sculpture, but in the increasing massiveness of furniture, the over-loading of ornament, the elaboration of dress and coiffure. Garments become voluminous; even the King appears in fringed and pleated robes similar to those of Eastern potentates. Jewelry is massive; men as well as women now wear earrings, which are to become longer and showier as the New Kingdom nears its close. Heavy wigs of curls and plaits fixed with beeswax echo barbarous coiffures, today still in vogue among primitive tribes of the southland. Though the art and dress of Amunhotep's time retain some taste and restraint, in succeeding reigns they too often become merely vulgar.

As did every Egyptian who could afford to do so, Amunhotep III, while building his palace, took thought of his tomb. He had it constructed in a narrow gorge west of the royal burying ground, remote from those of his ancestors. It was naturally larger and more complex than any they had built, with a succession of pillared halls and numerous chambers opening from a twisting passageway hewn deep into the cliff. Though it was begun early in his reign, it was never finished. Only one of the four great halls and parts of the corridors were decorated with the customary scenes and magical texts taken from funerary papyri. Adjacent to the burial chamber of the King were two suites, which, contrary to all precedent, are thought to have been intended by the uxorious Pharaoh for his two Great Wives, Tiy and Sitamun.

Strangely enough, we know more about the lives of the workmen who built Amunhotep's tomb than we do about that of the King himself. These men lived in a village founded by early rulers of the Eighteenth Dynasty, the remains of which, uncovered by modern archaeologists, have yielded an intimate knowledge of the families that dwelt in it. It was a walled village, hidden in a desolate hollow of the desert plateau, not far from the entrance to the Valley of the Kings. The men who inhabited it had as sole occupation the hewing and decoration of royal tombs and proudly bore the title of "Servitors in the Place of Truth." Like the hamlet of necropolis workers at Amarna, it was remote from cultivation and entirely lacking in water, and it was closely guarded—its inhabitants were all but prisoners, detained in the narrow confines of their desert valley. Founded probably when Ineni built the first of the Tombs of the Kings for his master, Thutmose I, it endured for almost five hundred years, until the last of the frayed line of the Ramessides had been laid to rest. Its ancient name is unknown, but today it is called Deir el Medineh, after an adjacent convent where Christian monks sought peace in the desolate valley.

From the deserted houses of the village, from tombs its craftsmen built for themselves in the surrounding cliffs, most of all from rubbish heaps rich in discarded records written on scraps of papyrus, potsherds, and limestone flakes, archaeologists have been able to reconstruct the lives of its ancient inhabitants in astonishing detail. Their names indicate that they were a mixed lot of Nubian, Asiatic, and Egyptian descent, apparently originally recruited from among captives or the half-assimilated descendants of captives and natives of lowly origin. In the beginning, the villagers were few; but when Amunhotep III built his tomb, the population had increased so as to require fifty houses within the walls and additional dwellings clustered beyond them. The male inhabitants formed a corporation or guild, in which a man was classified according to his work. At the head stood the directors of works, architects, foremen, and scribes; then came the artists—draftsmen, sculptors, and painters; next in rank were artisans—quarrymen and masons; finally, the common laborers—diggers and mortar mixers and porters of materials and water. The lowest rank of all were the persons who supplied the needs of the village itself—the washermen and watchmen, the donkey men who brought food and fuel and water.

Those who worked on the royal tombs were divided into

gangs, each serving for a ten-day period. As tombs were constructed in more and more remote places, a rest station was built in a pass above the village, where in rather miserable shelters each shift spent its nights, returning home only when its ten-day stint was finished. All of the workers, regardless of rank, were paid in kind, in this differing not at all from craftsmen and laborers employed elsewhere in Thebes or in Egypt as a whole. Though these villagers formed an aristocracy among workers, directly dependent on the King and probably better—and usually more regularly—paid than the average worker, the annual wage of a craftsman was about equal to the price of a single ox. Each month a meticulous accounting of work and hours was presented at a royal temple of the Theban necropolis, there to be checked by scribes and paid in food and other necessities. Each month a train of donkeys brought to the villagers their allotments of bread and beer (staples for all classes), beans and onions and fat, dried meat and fish and salt, together with work supplies such as colors and tools.

All this can be learned from accounts on ostraca discarded by village scribes. The ostraca also tell of absences from work and the frequently specious excuses for absence, of the quarrels and scandals inevitable in any hamlet and especially in one so confined. To the modern archaeologists who have studied the records, these ancient people have become neighbors about whom they can exchange news and gossip. It is possible to trace the careers of some of the families through many generations. As elsewhere in Egypt, sons usually followed the crafts of their fathers; but occasionally, through ability or diligence (or sometimes favor), a man could rise above the estate to which he had been born.

Such a man was the architect Kha, who started life as a draftsman and became successively a scribe and an architect, honored by Amunhotep II, Thutmose IV, and Amunhotep III, the kings under whom he served. He was able to furnish a splendid tomb for himself in his native valley, the contents of which are now in the Turin Museum. They include, together with wooden household furniture and textiles tapestry woven in colored patterns (rarely found in any tomb, however splendid), a beautiful ebony statuette of Kha himself, still wearing a garland of once-fresh flowers; and among the treasures he took with him to eternity were royal gifts, one of them a cup of white gold bearing the name of Amunhotep III.

Rank brought the villagers honor and added income, but it did not mean larger or better quarters. The houses crowded within the walls of Deir el Medineh were about the same for all. That of Kha was hardly larger than those of his neighbors. The village was traversed from gate to gate by a street scarcely three feet broad, from which a lane led to a second street running along one wall. Bordering these two ways, the houses were built on the same plan, like modern "company" tenements, wall to wall and back to back, each a bare fifteen feet wide, about twice as long, and about ten feet high. A typical plan showed four small rooms: an entrance hall, which served also as a utility room and workroom, a living room with a single pillar, a bedroom, and a kitchen. The entrance hall was usually lighted only by the street door; the living room, higher than the others, had slits in the clerestory to serve as windows; the bedroom that led from it had no light at all; and the kitchen more often than not was open to the sky. A stairway led to the flat roof, which served as a much-needed extra room; another led downward to a minuscule storage cave. When one walks through the village today or stands within the crumbled walls of an excavated dwelling, one feels like a Gulliver in a Lilliputian hamlet. It is difficult to imagine swarming families living and working in the tiny houses or a jostling holiday crowd in a street hardly wide enough to allow passage for a loaded donkey.

In reality, the houses of Deir el Medineh were probably more ample and better built than those of most of the common people of Amunhotep's time. They were superior to those of many modern villagers. Like their ancestors, the majority of today's fellahin live in tiny dwellings made of sun-dried brick, with floors of beaten earth and roofs of branching stems plastered over with mud. An adobe house can be a very pleasant home, but those of many Egyptians are tumbledown and crowded, with no more in the way of modern conveniences than the houses of three thousand years ago. Like the dwellings of Deir el Medineh, they are sparsely furnished. The meager possessions of the average householder of the ancient village consisted of a single rude bedstead or, more often of sleeping mats to be tossed on the floor or mud brick divan, a few stone stools, a low table or two, a modest battery of pottery bowls and jars, a mortar for grinding grain, a flat slab for kneading dough, and a domed clay oven for baking it. Among such goods a villager of the present would feel at home and, on the whole, rather well off.

The architect Kha furnished his tomb with much finer things than these. It is doubtful that he could have crowded into his small house as much as was packed into his last home, but—as so often—his burial equipment may have represented what he hoped for in a better world rather than what he had enjoyed on earth. The furniture found in his tomb showed little sign of use, and most of it was simply a painted mockery of the elaborately inlaid chairs and tables and chests fashioned of fine woods for his betters. That furniture skillfully inlaid in ivory and faïence and colored glass was made by craftsmen of the village is evident from the debris found in those rooms of their houses which doubled as workshops. Such debris also contains designs for various household objects, molds for jewelry, flawed pieces that testify to the manufacture of faïence, and fragments of unfinished sculptures; but whether the village craftsmen worked for themselves and their neighbors or chiefly for more distinguished patrons is unclear. It can be assumed that the fine ebony statuette of Kha was made locally, and it and other beautifully fashioned objects found on the site indicate that there were gifted artists among the villagers.

Certainly the tombs which the Servitors in the Place of Truth built for themselves were handsomely decorated. Few artists and craftsmen working elsewhere in Thebes could aspire to burials as fine as those on which the workers of Deir el Medineh employed their leisure and, undoubtedly, the royal tools and colors. They lavished their skill not only on themselves, but on the gods as well. Each category of the corporation built outside the walls a shrine to its guardian deity, and a well-preserved Ptolemaic temple today marks the site of an earlier shrine that the villagers dedicated to Hathor.

Like all other Egyptians, the inhabitants of Deir el Medineh were pious. Directly and proudly dependent upon the ruling king, they venerated the great gods of the capital, especially Amun, whom they approached (particularly after the Amarna schism) in a curiously personal way, inscribing on ostraca touching prayers addressed to him as "vizier of the poor" and "judge who taketh not bribes." Osiris, god and judge of the dead, they naturally venerated, though Isis, the divine mother, and Hathor in her dual capacity as goddess of love and of the cemetery, were closer to them. Ptah, the master craftsman, and the wise Thoth, patron of scribes and draftsmen and architects, had many worshipers; and on household shrines appeared the comfortable minor divinities never honored with temples of their own, the good Bes and the grotesque hippopotamus goddess Tauret, protectress of women in childbirth.

The chief god of the villagers, however, was the deified King Amunhotep I, whom they worshiped as founder of their corporation. They pictured him accompanied by his mother, Nofretari (who, being mother of Horus-the-King, was identified with Isis-Hathor), and also by Anubis, the jackal-embalmer and guardian of the cemetery. It was chiefly to the royal pair that the villagers brought their problems. The divine Amunhotep I by oracle decided their quarrels over property, identified thieves, acted as arbiter in cases of disputed payment, heard appeals from the decisions of the village tribunal. From the village his cult gradually spread to other sanctuaries of Western Thebes, and of all the royal ancestors, he was venerated the longest, unforgotten even in the time of the Ptolemies. Today his name, garbled and unrecognized as such, is perpetuated in a month of the Coptic calendar, which was inherited from the pharaohs and is only now dying out of general use.

Though the inhabitants of Deir el Medineh were a class apart, their village was not dissimilar to the many other villages that made up greater Thebes; and the lives they led were, on the whole, typical of the lives of the Theban masses over whom the magnificent Amunhotep III ruled. Only a handful of Egyptians could aspire to much more than a bare subsistence. Most of the others accepted the estate to which they had been born. They were content to work the day long for a meager fare, glad of a hovel to shelter themselves and their animals (if they were so lucky as to own any), thankful to receive at rare intervals coarse linen for a single garment, happy to participate in the many festivals of the Egyptian year—festivals that meant pageantry and music, often an extra ration from the bounty of god or king.

The masses were probably as well off toward the close of the Eighteenth Dynasty as they have been at any other time in history, almost certainly better off than they are today. Some among them were ambitious, and now and then a man of humble birth managed to rise in the world, but few hankered after things that were beyond their station in life. They complained sometimes, they tried to evade the tax collector and occasionally fled conscription, but they did not question the right of king or overlord to their persons and the products of their toil. That right was part of the order of the universe.

Thebes, like any other city of any other time or place, had its restless and rebellious spirits, its skeptics, its cheats and malefactors and criminals. Quick-flaring quarrels sometimes resulted in mayhem or murder. Thieves were abroad by night, and footpads lurked along desolate ways. Even the well-policed necropolis was occasionally invaded by robbers, who secretly burrowed into richly furnished tombs, sometimes (as tomb robbers do today) hacking out the eyes of figures depicted on the walls so that their guilt might not be witnessed. On the whole, however, during the prosperous and orderly reign of Amunhotep III, misdemeanors among the people were petty and few. The masses accepted the world as it was and hoped for at least as good a world after death.

The rare records that give glimpses of popular life reveal that the hardworking Thebans, like their modern Upper Egyptian descendants, were merry and possessed of a ready wit. They sang at their tasks and in their idle hours spun folk tales full of marvels. Only fragments of their songs and sayings and stories have come down to us; most of them were never written. So, at the present time, an oral literature that still exists among the fellahin (some of it perhaps of great antiquity) is rapidly being submerged in a flood of modernity, with only traces of it recorded.

CHAPTER FOUR

Amunhotep the Magnificent

WHAT MANNER OF MAN was Amunhotep III, and what was the life he led in his "House of Rejoicing?" Many and grandiloquent as the records of his reign are, the answers to these questions must be looked for between the lines.

It is hard not to picture the King as he appears in a late and undoubtedly faithful portrait from Amarna, which shows him with bloated face and sagging body, listless and weary. Earlier and more conventional portraits represent him, however, as a rather coarsely handsome youth, thick necked, full lipped, and almond eyed, not very sensitive nor perhaps very intelligent, but full of healthy vigor. So he must have looked when he inherited the throne of the Two Lands.

He was only about fifteen, but in ancient Egypt a youth of fifteen was a man. There is every reason to believe that he was already married to the little nobody named Tiy, daughter of one of his mother's attendants and perhaps a childhood sweetheart, who was destined to become his Great Royal Wife. He had received, no doubt at Memphis, the customary education of princes, a modicum of book learning and religious lore and a strenuous drilling in the manly arts of war and the chase. During the early years of his reign, he was active in the immemorial sport of kings. He issued for distribution among his favorites handsome souvenirs in the form of large scarabs vaunting his prowess as a hunter. One of them celebrated a two-day hunt in which he brought down with his own arrows 86 savage bulls (commandeering a whole garrison to serve as beaters), and another vaingloriously recorded that he had killed 102 fierce lions during his first ten years on the throne.

In the Egypt of his day, game was not as plentiful as it had been in olden times. Wild cattle were still to be found in the Eastern Desert, but lions were harder to come by. Though it has been suggested that Amunhotep may have gone as far afield as the Euphrates valley in search of them, he might well have found them nearer home, still lurking in reedy lairs of the Delta or near the sparse waterholes of the eastern mountains, or certainly in Nubia, where they were then abundant and have been almost down to our own time. It is more than likely, however, that the royal hunts took place in the King's own well-stocked game preserves.

After his tenth year there is no evidence that Amunhotep ever again engaged in strenuous sports, and he never campaigned at the head of his troops as his illustrious forefathers had done. Though his inscriptions echo the juster claims of his predecessors to Asiatic conquest, sometimes borrowing their very words, he apparently never set foot in Syria ("Verily, thy father did not march forth nor inspect the lands of his vassal princes," wrote a Syrian ruler to Amunhotep's son); and there is even doubt that he led in person the one insignificant expedition to Nubia reported in his fourth year, though he boasted of having crushed the "vile Kushites" on a number of victory stelae and made a triumphal progress almost to the Fourth Cataract, bringing back a tribute of gold to his father Amun.

The times were against him. The machinery of government

set in motion by former kings seemed to run smoothly. Subject peoples, mindful of former punishment, were temporarily docile. Tribute (though very often, now, in the form of "gifts" for which equal value was expected in return) continued to enrich the King and his god. The abundant Nile unfailingly sent down its annual flood; the gold mines seemed inexhaustable. Egypt prospered as never before and was at peace. There was little apparent need for a ruler to exert himself. By the time he was twenty-five or so, Amunhotep had become a lazy, luxury-loving, Oriental potentate, and so he remained to the end of his days.

Sculptures from Thebes, possibly made when he was around fifty, show him as obese, effeminately clad in an elaborately pleated and fringed robe, his hands clasped below his protruding belly in a characteristically Eastern gesture. Such statutes are a far cry from the dignified virility of the representations of former kings, but life in Egypt was no longer what it had been in olden days. The mores of the court and the upper classes had been gradually corrupted by too great prosperity, too great familiarity with less austere societies. People realized, now, that there was another world beyond the boundaries of Egypt. Many had traveled abroad as soldiers or officials or merchants, bringing back tales, which undoubtedly lost nothing in the telling, of exotic lands and of peoples whose ways, from their very strangeness, seemed freer and more colorful than those of the homeland. Homesick slaves in great houses told the women and children of the wealth and beauty of other lands, ruled by other kings and other gods.

Tomb paintings of the late Eighteenth Dynasty reveal very clearly a laxity of manners, an ostentation of luxury once foreign to Egyptian life. In earlier scenes, men had partaken of the funerary meal in hieratic dignity, alone or in the company of staid wives, with children and servants in respectful attendance. Now, too often, that solemn meal reflects a revel, with many guests partaking of the viands offered to the dead and drinking to the point of drunkenness. Slender, nude serving maids heap mounds of scented ointments on convivial heads. Men and women, elaborately gowned and bejeweled and bewigged, languidly sniff lotus flowers as they watch half-veiled girls twisting in sensuous dances and listen to singers who chant reckless songs to the music of instruments borrowed from the East.

> "Odors and oils for thy nostrils,
> Wreaths of lotus for thy beloved
> Who is beside thee and in thy heart . . .
> Let us have song and music!
> Come pleasure—away with care!
> For the day dawneth when we draw near
> The land that loveth silence."

To modern ears, the name of Amunhotep's palace, the "House of Rejoicing," suggests similar revels. Though it was, on the contrary, a solemnly religious name, given to his palace by the King on the occasion of his first jubilee to signify rejoicing in the renewal of his kingship, the Pharaoh may nevertheless have taken his pleasure in ways not dissimilar to those depicted in the tombs of his courtiers. Feasting and the entertainment provided by the musicians and dancing girls of his entourage certainly were among his diversions, though the royal revels may have been dampened by formality and restraint.

Kings can rarely allow themselves boon companions. While

a few of the men who proudly bore the title of "Intimate of the King" possibly had some claim to that precarious honor, and the Pharaoh may have permitted himself to unbend a bit in their company or in the privacy of the harem, freedom could have been only on one side; and it is doubtful that Amunhotep ever enjoyed much real companionship save perhaps that of the wife of his youth, Tiy, who remained his confidant and friend. Of her, more later.

Too much above the run of mankind to be anything but lonely, the Pharaoh could find satisfaction in his power and the splendor of it, in the edifices into which he poured his wealth, and in the homage he received. From time to time he showed himself in majesty to the obsequious envoys of foreign princes, who prostrated themselves before his throne. On occasion, he received in state the great of his realm, who came, bending low, to present sumptuous gifts for the New Year or the anniversary of his coronation or the celebration of his jubilee—statues in his own likeness, furniture and jewelry, fine linen, precious vessels fashioned in the workshops under their supervision, or provisions and vintage wines from the estates they controlled through his bounty. From the "Window of Appearances," overlooking a courtyard of his palace, he distributed decorations of golden chains and bracelets to men he wished to honor. On the occasion of the great festivals, he went in glittering pomp to consort with the gods in their temples; as he passed, an awed populace groveled in the dust.

But it is not altogether easy to be an absolute monarch, and Amunhotep had other, more onorous duties to perform. As King of Egypt, he not only headed the state: he was the state. His edicts were its law. He himself appointed the chief government officials who acted in his stead, the high priests who served as his proxies. Theoretically, and sometimes actually, he appointed minor officials and clergy as well. Since he not only made these men but could also break them (and sometimes did), no official in his right mind could dare to take any important action or embark on any project without his sanction. Such sanction might be capriciously given or arbitrarily withheld, but it was necessary; and so the King had at intervals to receive in audience his vizier and other important functionaries to hear their reports, to instruct them in his wishes, and to seal their activities with his approval. Such audiences probably did not occur daily, as they are said to have occurred in the good old times, but they were necessarily frequent. Though Amunhotep may often have found them tedious, they could not have failed to add to his sense of power.

About the details of the government he controlled, the King probably knew little and cared less, and he concerned himself hardly at all with the toiling millions whose work filled the storehouses and granaries. Although we ourselves, looking back from the vantage point offered by time, can only dimly imagine the lives of those illiterate, voiceless masses, we have a little more knowledge of the complex administrative system under which they were governed. It was, for its time, a highly evolved system, and one that, in spite of the vicissitudes of revolution and war and foreign occupation, endured into the Ptolemaic period with surprisingly little fundamental change. Indeed, in essence, grown rusty with archaism, it was handed down almost to our own time. For what we know of the system we are dependent chiefly upon a large and very miscellaneous collection of documents penned by the ancient scribes who kept the records of government.

The administration employed thousands of clerks. In pictured scenes these clerks are omnipresent, here surveying the fields, recording the measuring of grain and the counting of cattle, collecting the taxes due to the king; there, numbering recruits to the army or the *corvée*; everywhere, standing obsequious at the elbows of their betters with ready papyrus scrolls and reed pens. The surviving results of their labors are overwhelming. Almost from the time when writing was first invented, administrative records had been made in Egypt and carefully preserved, but during the Empire, with the increasing complexity of government, the archives were filled to bursting. No ancient civilization, perhaps no modern civilization excepting our own, was ever as paper-ridden as that of Egypt.

Many documents that have come down to us still lie in museums unstudied. The great number that have been translated by scholars are an ill-assorted lot, stemming from widely scattered places and different times. They are often fragmentary, not rarely incomprehensible. Scraps of accounts, lists of lands and slaves and cattle, tax registers, inventories of temple goods and properties, court records, most often concerned with petty disputes and comparatively rarely with cases of importance, deeds and contracts, a few literary works, and great masses of religious texts—it is from such things, recorded on papyrus or sherds or limestone flakes, that Egyptologists have pieced together an idea of the civilization of the New Kingdom. They supplement the knowledge thus gained with a few royal edicts and with records (not always trustworthy) of kingly conquests and achievements engraved on stone, a few biographical inscriptions, a meticulous, compara-

tive study of the titles borne by ancient officials. Last, but by
no means least, they can draw on unwritten history as represented in the monuments, the pictured scenes in tombs, the
relics of daily life buried with the dead or surviving in the
debris of settlements.

While a surprising number of the available clerkly documents are exceedingly well written, some are from the hands
of barely literate scribes; many others are the work of schoolboys struggling with archaic or "highfalutin" language remote
from their common speech. It was no easy task to learn to
write correctly. The sacred hieroglyphs invented by Thoth,
the scribe of the gods, were pictures, often confusingly similar. To draw them accurately required more than a little
skill. In the cursive hieratic writing derived from them, a
slight carelessness, a false stroke could alter the meaning of a
word and a sentence. The number of signs to be learned was
staggering. There was no such thing as a simple alphabet of
twenty-six letters of more or less fixed phonetic value, which
could be used to express in writing the thought and speech of a
people. In the time of Amunhotep III, a learned scribe had to
have at his command about six hundred symbols; in later
periods, the number of signs employed was even greater.
The road to learning was not easy, but it was open to many,
and every ambitious Egyptian longed to set foot upon the way.

A papyrus from Thebes dating from shortly after the reign
of Amunhotep III praises learning for its own sake. "Be a
scribe," it says, "that thy name may live. Better is a book than
a tomb in the West . . . better than a stela in a temple." It
tells of great men of the past whose mortuary rites have been
long neglected, whose tombs have crumbled into dust, the

very sites forgotten, "but their names are still pronounced because of the books they made" and will "last to the limits of eternity."

This is a rare document. Most scribes were interested far less in literary immortality than in immediate advancement. A scribe's career could lead far. Great men were proud to include the title of scribe in their lists of honors, and many of them had risen from the obscure post of humble clerk to exalted position. Even the scribe who could never advance beyond employment in a provincial office or on a small estate was an effendi, whose garments were white. Thus most of the documents that extol a scribe's career emphasize its merits in terms of material advantage. They paint the lives of farmers and craftsmen, of traders and soldiers in the gloomiest of colors and depict the life of the scribe in brilliant contrast. "Be a scribe," they urge in essence. "Be diligent. Act with discretion and modesty toward your superiors. Never question an order, never speak out of turn. Then you will not lack for food 'from the property of the House of the King.'" Such are the copybook maxims assigned to schoolboys of the New Kingdom.

We speak of schoolboys. Actually, the scribe received the greater part of his education through an arduous apprenticeship. After being taught the "three R's" at home or in a primary school, where instruction was often to the tune of a stick, for "a boy's ear is on his back," the prospective scribe continued his education as an apprentice in a government or estate office or in a temple scriptorium.

Learning was by practice. It consisted of interminable copying, endless memorizing of individual signs, words and groups of words, model letters, excerpts from the classics.

Even arithmetic meant committing to memory typical examples, for no one, apparently, had ever reasoned out the basic principles of mathematics. Scribes learned to keep accurate accounts and to compute cubic volumes, architects planned and engineers raised the great Theban temples that have lasted for three millennia or more with small mathematical equipment beyond a rudimentary geometry and a simple arithmetic that knew neither multiplication nor division (both were arrived at tediously by way of addition and subtraction) and employed only the most elementary of fractions. Moreover, the monuments that can still cause wonder in an age of skyscrapers were erected with few mechanical aids, and those of the simplest. No great cranes, not so much as a block and tackle; only hundreds of human hands.

Egyptian education produced great men—wise administrators, learned priests, gifted architects and artists, writers, poets, and a host of able clerks—but in essence it was static. It did not seek to develop reasoning nor to inspire intellectual curiosity. There was nothing to be curious about. The world was as it was in the beginning and always would be. Its phenomena had long since been satisfactorily explained. Every innovation had to be fitted into the established framework. From among the products of this tradition-bound education were chosen the men who governed Egypt in the name of the king. They were divided into three dominant factions—the civil service, the army, and the clergy. While the Twelfth Dynasty had witnessed the emergence of a fairly substantial middle class, there was hardly anything that could be called such in the New Kingdom. There was merely a governing class and the rest. Artists and craftsmen, merchants and small farmers, all the men who might have constituted a solid bourgeoisie were simply adjuncts to one or another of the three factions. Like the serfs who tilled the fields, they were paid in kind and differed from serfs chiefly in the superior honor and greater emoluments attached to their callings. The three factions were mutually jealous and potential rivals for power. Only faith in the established order as embodied in the kingship could hold them in check. Under the weak pharaohs of later times, the army and the priesthood gained control.

For this, not only Amunhotep III but also his predecessors paved the way. The rulers of the Eighteenth Dynasty had lavished lands and treasure upon the Theban Amun until his riches rivaled those of the throne. His chief priests, sharing the divine luxury, had sumptuous dwellings, landed properties, and slaves of their own. By making Amun state god and king of all the gods, the pharaohs had put all the other divinities of Egypt, their priests, their worshipers, and their temples under Theban control. A Theban official, frequently the High Priest of Amun, was "Overseer of All the Priests of the Two Lands." Small wonder that the clergy of Karnak might see themselves as defenders of the faith—preservers, incidentally, of the *status quo*.

On the other hand, the warrior kings of the Eighteenth Dynasty had to an ever greater extent rewarded their gallant army officers with high posts in the administration. They had taken their former companions-at-arms into their households in positions of trust or intimacy. They had even bestowed clerical livings on veterans. Though these military men, distributed throughout the government, formed a clique of their own almost as powerful as the entrenched priesthood of Amun, Amunhotep III could still maintain control. The very fact that government in his reign was an interlocking directorate, with retired army officers holding civil and clerical positions, priests in the civil service, and, conversely, civil servants in posts of ecclesiastical dignity, lent strength to the throne. So long as no one faction was permitted to gain the upper hand, the dynastic succession seemed assured.

Under Amunhotep III, as had long been customary, the vizier was second in command to the king. While a courtier, such as Amunhotep, son of Hapu, onetime Scribe of Recruits, may have stood higher in royal favor and wielded greater influence than the vizier, the functions of the latter had, on the whole, changed little from the time of Thutmose III, when Rekhmire recorded his duties and accomplishments on the walls of his tomb, in a text borrowed from the Middle Kingdom. In the name of the pharaoh, the vizier watched over every department of the government. He exchanged reports with the treasurer, kept an eye on royal workshops and storehouses. He supervised the priests and the estates of the temples, acted as secretary of war and navy, controlled internal defense and (at least to some extent) conscription, made minor appointments, both civil and ecclesiastical. His office was responsible for cadastral surveys, regulated the assessment and collection of taxes. He himself presided over the supreme court. He was custodian of state and legal archives, keeper of deeds and contracts. As vizier of the South, he was usually ex-officio mayor of Thebes, and at least one of Amunhotep's Southern viziers, Ptahhotep, was also High Priest of Amun. Of the vizier of the North, we know less, but his functions probably differed little from those of his Upper Egyptian counterpart.

The early kings of the Eighteenth Dynasty had eliminated the nomarchs, those hereditary nobles who, as provincial governors, had proved to be so troublesomely independent in the past. They were replaced by the mayors of the principal cities of Upper and Lower Egypt. It has been said that the civilization of Egypt was a "civilization without cities." Towns of some size, however, remotely comparable to the cathedral towns of early medieval Europe, had grown up around the most important temples, and it was in such centers, frequently the ancient nome capitals, that the seats of local government were established. Some of the provincial mayors appointed by Thebes were descended from the old nobility, but the majority, though they often claimed the title of "Hereditary Prince and Count," were political appointees, retired army officers, or relations of Theban dignitaries. These men were sometimes incompetent, not rarely corruptible, but their activities, controlled by the central administration, were strictly limited to local affairs. They were responsible for the maintenance of the irrigation works of their districts, prob- ably also for the recruiting of the *corvées* that maintained them, and for the collection of taxes. They presided over the local courts.

The ancient Egyptian legal and judicial system, like many other aspects of government, was well organized and sur- prisingly advanced. No written code has come down to us, but there is reason to believe that such a code existed and that the king, who was the law, respected its precedents and only rarely exercised in an arbitrary manner his absolute power over the property and persons of his subjects. Even men who plotted against the throne were condemned only after trial. The humblest peasant could appeal to the supreme court pre- sided over by the vizier and in extremity could carry his grievance to the pharaoh. Such, at least, was the ideal. In practice things rarely worked that way. A poor man without influence was wise to avoid the law. He was lucky if he could obtain a just decision from a local court, luckier still if he could reach the tribunal of the vizier. In far-off patriarchal times, it had perhaps been possible to gain the ear of the king; it is doubtful that a humble plaintiff ever was permitted access to the magnificent Amunhotep III.

The "Tale of the Eloquent Peasant," written in the Twelfth Dynasty, perhaps as an admonition to magistrates, shows that then the servant of a rich official could rob a poor peasant with impunity and that the complaint of the victim might be met only with the bastinado. The hero of the tale voiced his protest boldly: "Do not plunder a poor man, a weakling, of his property—that is his very breath of life. You were appointed to judge between two men, but behold, you favor the thief. One trusts you, but you have become the culprit. . . . You have everything you need; your belly is full. . . . Takers, robbers, confiscators—magistrates! And it is you who are made to punish evil!"

In storybook fashion the peasant talked himself to the notice of the king and was rewarded tenfold for the loss he had suffered. In real life, the result of such eloquence might be very different. While there were undoubtedly just magistrates and just decisions in the courts of the New Kingdom, bribery was rife and the use of the bastinado frequent. Even witnesses were beaten. Punishments were severe. One hundred strokes, sometimes with added infliction of wounds, was not a rare penalty. Major offenders might have their ears or noses cut off or be sent to exile in mines or quarries or in bleak desert outposts. That both mutilation and exile could be their lot is indicated by the name of a dreary garrison on

the road to Asia, which the Greeks dubbed "Rhinocorura"—
"Cut-off-Noses." The death penalty was comparatively rare,
and it could be pronounced only by the king. In the case of
high-placed offenders, a benevolent sovereign sometimes miti-
gated it by giving the culprit a choice between execution and
suicide.

Though justice was on occasion not only blind but deaf,
the Egyptians remained incorrigibly litigious. Legal documents penned by the ancient scribes record endless petty disputes over land and water rights and inheritances, endless
complaints of extortion, thievery, and assault. To give the
magistrates their due, their task was far from easy. Plaintiff
and defendant presented conflicting testimony under oath,
and it was for the court to decide which was perjuring himself. In spite of beatings, witnesses swore falsely. The loser of
a case had to be bound, under threat of physical punishment,
to abide by the decision of the judges. The wonder is that a
rough justice was ever achieved, but achieved it was, sometimes even when the defendants were persons of prominence.

Many legal records as well as innumerable administrative
documents have to do with taxation. In fact, one can hardly
avoid the idea that the levying and collection of taxes was
the major activity of government. Everything in Egypt was
taxed, but the wealth of the country and, consequently, the
chief source of income for the state derived from the land;
and it can not be said too often that all the land, quite literally,
belonged to the king.

The theory of royal ownership has been known in many
countries, including those of the West, but in Egypt theory
remained practice almost to the present time. A hundred years
ago, Lady Lucie Duff-Gordon, slowly dying in her house

among the ruins of Amunhotep's temple at Luxor, where she lived among the peasantry, beloved by them and venerated almost as a saint, could write indignantly: "The whole land belongs to the Sultan of Turkey, the Pasha being his vakeel (representative). . . . Thus there are no owners, only tenants paying from one hundred piastres (£1) down to thirty piastres yearly per *feddan* (about an acre) according to the quality of the land, or the favor of the Pasha when granting it. This tenancy is hereditary to children—not to collaterals or ascendents—and it may be sold, but in that case application must be made to the Government. If the owner or tenant dies childless the land reverts to the Sultan, i.e., to the Pasha, and *if the Pasha chooses to have any man's land he can take it from him on payment—or without.* Don't let anyone tell you I exaggerate; I have known it to happen: I mean the *without*, and the man received feddan for feddan of desert in return for his good land which he has tilled or watered." (*Letters from Egypt,* London, 1902, 202).

In the time of Amunhotep III, at least a third, and possibly more, of the productive land was directly under the crown; almost as much belonged to the temples, predominant among them the temple of Amun at Karnak; the remainder was divided into larger or smaller estates, which were held in fief by persons who enjoyed the favor of the throne. A very few tracts were cultivated by small farmers, who tilled them independently with the aid of their families. Crown and temple properties and great estates were worked by serfs or slaves under the direction of stewards or overseers or were parceled out to free tenant farmers, who cultivated them on shares.

To be included in the crown (or state) lands were the considerable areas allotted to the queen and other members of the royal family for their personal use, those assigned to the royal harem, and those whose products, together with gifts and other perquisites of office, went into the privy purse of the reigning king. Through the generations vast tracts had been set aside as endowments for the maintenance of the temples and cults of departed rulers. These endowments were under the control of the living monarch; and while most kings hesitated to encroach on the properties of the great gods, those of the ancestors were frequently held less sacrosanct. Especially the mortuary temples of discredited or unimportant rulers, who no longer lived in popular veneration, were allowed to fall into ruin, their rites neglected, their incomes— often their very stones—diverted to the use of the living pharaoh.

Although royal endowments of lands for the tombs and funerary cults of private persons, those "boons of the king" so frequently given to courtiers of the past, had necessarily (as a result of increasing population and shortage of tillable land) dwindled into an all but empty formula, a *main morte* still lay heavy on the economy. Great sums were expended for the building and furnishing of private tombs, and privately held property was set aside to endow them. As if the royal bounty to the temples of the gods and deified kings were not sufficient, officials added to it by endowments of their own, in the hope of currying favor not only with the gods, but also with the pharaoh. One such official in the reign of Amunhotep III endowed a statute of the King in the latter's mortuary temple at Memphis because, as he frankly stated in his own tomb, he had grown rich through his sovereign's bounty. This official was, incidentally, another Amunhotep, of Memphite origin, who tells of a career almost as spectacular as that of the son of Hapu. He was apparently of even humbler birth than the latter, but he, too, advanced to be a Scribe of Recruits, royal architect, and, finally, Chief Steward of the Pharaoh's Memphite estates ("My stick," he says, "was on the heads of the people!"). He was able, out of his wealth, to donate almost three hundred acres to his King's "living image."

Although all property belonged to the king, private ownership was (as has already been suggested) relatively stable. Holders, after due formalities, could sell their property or bequeath it. Even tenancies were inheritable; stewardships, like other offices, sometimes remained in the same families for generations. It is true that if a man fell from royal favor, his lands could be confiscated. A change of regime, and especially a change of dynasty, almost inevitably resulted in some painful reallocation of ownership. But on the whole, kings and nobles prided themselves on "robbing no man of his inheritance," and, excepting in times of great crisis, the economy of the land remained undisturbed.

All land, all flocks and herds, all serfs and slaves were taxable. Though certain exemptions were granted in the case of temple property, even the fields of the gods rendered their tithes to the king. The tenant farmers, whether they worked private lands or temple or crown lands, were taxed on the shares they received in return for their labor. While taxes were apparently based on the estimated rather than the actual yield, an attempt was made to distribute the burden fairly. The law distinguished between agricultural and grazing lands, between poor and fertile fields, floodlands and artificially irrigated holdings, well-established and newly reclaimed tracts. Natural disaster, such as failure of the inundation, meant a reduction in taxes. In extreme need, farmers were given grain for next season's sowing and food was distributed from temple and royal storehouses.

It will readily be seen that so complex a system of land tenure and taxation had to rest on a census of population, a counting of cattle and herds, and frequent cadastral surveys to check the areas under cultivation and to re-establish boundaries obliterated by the annual flood. Recording was complicated by the fact that few large landholders held a single bloc of territory. Royal and temple estates and those of the landed gentry were made up of widely scattered parcels of agricultural and grazing lands, gardens and vineyards. Much of the crown land and a considerable part of that held by Amun of Karnak was distributed through the rich Delta, which offered, among other desirable properties, suitable pasturage for cattle, vast numbers of which were needed for sacrificial purposes alone. Many wealthy Thebans had holdings here and there in Lower Egypt, and, conversely, Lower Egyptians owned tracts in the Nile Valley. Such distribution of property in small allotments was perhaps due in part to the geographical idiosyncracies of the country, though it had the advantage that no single powerful owner could control in its entirety any considerable region and the people inhabiting it.

Bookkeeping for tax purposes was further complicated by the fact that all taxes were paid in kind. This meant that vast quantities of grain and produce, cattle and other livestock, manufactured articles of all kinds had to be collected locally, stored for shipment, and ultimately delivered to royal granaries and storehouses, from where they were distributed for the use of the army, government employees, and the king's vast household, and for the royal trading ventures. The royal treasurer was a very important official, for he and his agents were responsible for the receipt and distribution of these cumbersome payments. Scribes of the treasury swarmed through the land, checking the receipts at every stage of their journey.

"Tamper not with the scales," says a sage of the New Kingdom. "Conspire not with the corn-measurer." Almost everybody, up and down the line, was bent on defrauding the government. False declarations were made, figures juggled, measures rigged. The boatmen who carried grain to the storehouses pilfered their share. The tax collectors could be "fixed." As for the tenant farmer, whose "reckoning lasted to eternity," no one expected anything but cheating of him.

Popular literature and pictured scenes reveal that the peasant's tithe must frequently have been extracted from him with injustice and brutality. "Remember you not the condition of the cultivator faced with the registering of the harvest tax, when the snake has carried off half the grain and the hippopotamous has devoured the rest? The mice abound in the fields. The locusts descend. The cattle devour. The sparrows bring disaster. . . . What is left on the threshing floor . . . falls to the thieves. The yoke of oxen [as was common, probably leased by the farmer] has died while threshing and plowing. And now the scribe lands on the river-bank to register the harvest tax, with guards carrying staves and Nubian policemen carrying palm rods, and they say 'Hand over the grain' though there is none. The cultivator is beaten, he is bound and thrown into the well, head downward. His wife has been bound in his presence, and his children are in fetters. His

neighbors abandon him and are fled. Even so flees the grain."
(Adapted from Sir Alan H. Gardiner, *Journal of Egyptian
Archaeology,* Vol XXVII, [1941], 19–20.)

This dismal account from one of the many documents in
praise of the scribe's profession may be exaggerated, but it
doubtless had a foundation in bitter fact. The quotation ends
with the statement that "the scribe is ahead of everyone—he is
not taxed, has no dues to pay." But all others were taxed
directly or indirectly, and some were taxed doubly. The catch
of the fisherman, the bag of the hunter yielded their tithes.
A landowner paid on his serfs and slaves and on the products
of their work as well. Linen, papyrus, leather—all privately
manufactured articles—rendered dues in kind for the royal
magazines. Manufacture was usually on a small scale. While
relatively large workshops producing surpluses were attached
to palaces and temples and to great estates, there is evidence
that much manufacture was confined to filling individual
needs. Weavers occupied the *rez de chausées* of large houses,
villagers frequently had their own looms, many manu-
factures of popular use were products of cottage industry,
serving only the makers and their neighbors. Most trade,
except for petty transactions, was in the hands of the king
and the god Amun, both of whom had their caravans and
fleets. All other goods paid import and export duty, and mer-
chandise or produce carried up and down the Nile was subject to octrois.

How much direct taxation amounted to is a matter of pure
conjecture, though it is thought that the twenty per cent given
in Genesis (47:24, 26) may be approximately just. Even more
may have been obtained through indirect taxation. A form
of indirect taxation was the conscription of men for quarrying

and royal building projects. Privately owned boats, moreover, could be requisitioned for public use and by officials traveling on the king's business. Such officials expected free food and lodging for themselves and their escorts en route; and sometimes, as the records show, they illegally demanded transportation and hospitality when they journeyed for their own interest or pleasure. The home army and the police force were supported by the communities in which they were quartered, the foodstuffs and supplies furnished them being deducted from taxes due to the crown, but soldiers also occasionally commandeered services and supplies without authority. Finally, the "gifts" of produce and manufactured articles brought to His Majesty by his courtiers must be reckoned as indirect taxation, for they were expected tribute paid in return for royal favor.

Apparently almost no one was free of taxation except (if he can be believed) the scribe. He may have shared his blissful immunity with other landless persons, but he considered himself superior to these, for he could boast of clean garments and hands unsoiled by toil. His perquisites were often not much greater than those of many of the manual workers he was taught to despise. But he not infrequently might make a bit on the side, and if he were clever, he could speed his advancement by connivance or by little presents, judiciously placed.

There were upright officials in the time of Amunhotep III, but there is every reason to believe that the government was riddled with corruption. Those closest to the King could hardly fail to be aware of the all-too-human side of his dual nature, and among them were undoubtedly some who worked for their own profit, counting on their ruler's preoccupation with his pleasures. So long as they did not assume too much power and could avoid arousing the jealousy of their colleagues, they had a chance of enjoying illegal perquisites of office undetected. At the bottom of the scale, hundreds of ill-paid civil servants indulged in the age-old custom of petty graft, risking a beating or worse for the sake of added income. Provided the revenues of the crown were sufficient to maintain his splendor, the King remained indifferent.

In addition to the wealth yielded by the Two Lands and the Nubian colony, the royal treasury was enriched from the East. Asia offered many things that Egypt coveted—copper and silver, fine woods, horses, rare oils and wines, and luxury goods cunningly fashioned in foreign workshops. From vassal states came slaves, now needed as extra hands for agricultural work and construction, and exotic girls for the harems of King and courtiers ("Send me forty beautiful women," Amunhotep demanded in a letter to the Governor of Gezer; "no mischief-makers among them!"). A modicum of all these riches came to the Pharaoh as tribute; the remainder was acquired by trade, in exchange for leather and linen and papyrus, grain and handicrafts, ingots of gold. It was important for Egypt to maintain good relations with Asia; and, as was to be expected, it was the King himself who dictated Egypt's foreign policy. In his dealings with the East, Amunhotep III, unlike his ancestors, relied on diplomacy rather than arms. This was perhaps the result of royal inertia, but it may also have been an evidence of great wisdom; for powerful forces had arisen in Asia, open conflict with which might well have brought Egypt, for all its riches, to the point of ruin.

The correspondence of Amunhotep III with his royal "brothers" of Hither Asia, preserved on cuneiform tablets found among the state archives at Amarna, reveals that diplomacy three thousand or so years ago was, as often today, a polite word for bargaining. Peace was maintained in part by a show of strength (Egyptian governors and garrisons were still stationed at strategic points in Palestine and Syria), but chiefly by gold; and good relationships were cemented by matrimonial alliances. The eastern potentates were greedy. "Gold is as dust in the land of my brother," wrote the King of Mitanni to Amunhotep IV; and, indeed, gold poured into foreign lands as if it were a common thing, used openly to purchase allegiance, indirectly and for the same purpose as bride money for the daughters of foreign princes.

Early in his reign, Amunhotep took to wife a daughter of the King of Mitanni named Kirgipa and announced the marriage on one of his famous commemorative scarabs as "a marvel brought to His Majesty, the daughter of the Prince of Naharin [Mitanni] . . . and persons of her harem, 317 women." Shortly before his death, a second Mitannian princess was sent to the Pharaoh in the expectation that he would make her his Great Royal Wife and "mistress of Egypt," but the marriage was not consummated, and the exacting condition remained unfulfilled. In the meantime, however, Amunhotep had welcomed into his hospitable harem a daughter of the King of Arzawa and a daughter of the King of Babylonia, Kadashman-Enlil I.

The exchange of letters relating to the last-named bride is at once diverting and significant. When Amunhotep demanded the Princess to wife, Kadashman-Enlil dared counter with a request for a daughter of the Pharaoh. He was arrogantly and contemptuously refused: "From of old a daughter of a king of Egypt has not been given to Nobody." The Babylonian impudently replied, "Thou art a king. Thou canst do according to thy heart's desire. If thou givest, who can say anything?" And he sensibly added that any beautiful woman would have done, for "Who shall say she is not a king's daughter?" Though Kadashman-Enlil finally agreed to sell his own daughter to Amunhotep at a price, one wonders whether the wily Babylonian may not have turned the trick by substituting an anonymous beauty for his own flesh and blood.

Much of the foreign correspondence shows an easy familiarity toward the Pharaoh on the part of the Eastern princes. Some vassals still addressed him in extravagant terms: he was their god and their sun, they, the ground under his feet; but the diplomatic exchange reveals that the rulers of more important states regarded themselves as equals of the Egyptian King—his brothers. The way was open for a new great power, the Hittites, to seize control of Asia. Before the death of Amunhotep III, these Anatolian warriors had already conquered former Egyptian dependencies in northern Syria.

The Empire was tottering, and there was an undercurrent of unrest in Egypt itself. Whether the King was aware of it or remained insulated against it by his arrogance cannot be known. While most modern historians see Amunhotep III as indolent and indifferent, a lover of luxury and women, who, through sheer inertia, permitted land and empire to drift toward catastrophe, a few regard him and his son after him as embodiments of a progressive spirit seeking to combat the numbing traditionalism of the past. Certain scholars would divide the Egypt of the late Eighteenth Dynasty into a conservative party composed of priests and officials and a pro-

gressive party consisting of the army and military functionaries faithful to and headed by the King. It has been suggested
that Amunhotep's raising of the low-born Tiy to the position
of Great Royal Wife was a conscious and direct attack against
the reactionaries and the established religion, which demanded that a ruler marry his own sister, as alone eligible to
become God's Wife, to bear a son to Amun to inherit the
throne.

It is generally accepted that the Egyptian kingship was traditionally transmitted through the female line. A ruler was
hence bound to take as his Great Wife (his queen) a princess
of the blood royal, frequently, in the natural course of things,
his sister or half-sister. If one examines the line of the Eighteenth Dynasty, however, it becomes apparent that consan-
guineous marriages as often as not failed to produce an heir
to the throne and that in such a case the succession passed to
the son of a secondary wife (who may or may not have been
related to the royal family) or even to the son of a concubine.
This son usually bolstered his claim to the kingship by marriage to a half-sister or some other lady of irreproachable royal
lineage, whom he made his queen, and thus the eternal
illusion was sustained.

To state the matter more simply, a number of kings of the
Eighteenth Dynasty were of royal descent from only their
father's side, and Tiy was as eligible to bear an heir to the
throne as many another commoner had been. Amunhotep III
defied tradition only in making her his Great Royal Wife, a
title usually reserved for the sisters or daughters of kings.
His defiance may well have been a bland assumption of his
divine superiority rather than a conscious challenge to author-

ized religion and the conservative party. Late in his reign, he indeed married a princess of blood royal—his own daughter Sitamun, whom he made coequal with Tiy as his Great Queen, and who (or so some think) bore him two sons, Smenkhkare and Tutankhamun, who were destined to succeed Tiy's son Akhenaten in brief and ineffectual rule over the Two Lands. Whether this marriage was a sop to tradition or a symptom of senile concupiscence remains problematical.

In any event, there is small evidence that Amunhotep was inimical to the established faith or shared his son's vision of the Aten as sole god. He not only, as we have seen, publicly stressed his divine paternity, but he never failed in his devotion to his father Amun, erecting ever more splendid temples in his honor, lavishing costly gifts upon him, celebrating his festivals with an opulence hitherto unknown. The Aten, the disk of the sun, had long since been known to Egyptian theology. It was probably only to the visible manifestation of Re (or Amun-Re) that Amunhotep III erected a small shrine to the Disk in Karnak and named his palace and royal barge and a company of troops in honor of the Aten.

That the King may have been at least vaguely aware of some threat to the throne in ambitious and turbulent Thebes is possibly indicated by his choice of men to fill important posts in the government. Ever since the time of Thutmose III, the center of gravity of the country had been gradually shifting from Thebes to Memphis. More and more frequently representatives of Lower Egyptian families had been called to high office at the capital, but under Amunhotep III the chief positions, both lay and clerical, were placed almost exclusively in the hands of men from the North. Though this could hardly have been soothing to Theban families, many of which had

come to consider themselves as firmly in the saddle, whether
it was a sign of a progressive spirit on the part of the King is
questionable. It may have been in part the result of influence
brought to bear on the more or less indifferent monarch by
his favorite, the son of Hapu, who was a Lower Egyptian
by birth.

Like Senenmut long ago, Amunhotep, son of Hapu, seems
to have been a power behind the throne; his boast that he
was the "mouth"—the spokesman—of his ruler was probably
no mere conventional phrase. He was cannier than Senenmut,
for he held his ambitions in check, never "aspiring to high
office," but content to work quietly in positions of relatively
minor importance. The son of a provincial family of Athribis,
he began life as a scribe. According to his own account, it
was through his outstanding proficiency in the "holy words"
that he came to the notice of the King, who made him first
Royal Scribe and ultimately Chief Scribe of Recruits for
Lower Egypt. In the latter capacity, he reports, he not only
selected the fittest among the available young men for the
King's service, but also organized the defense of the Delta
frontiers. He owed his chief fame and probably his great
intimacy with the Pharaoh to his appointment as royal architect—Overseer of All the Works of the King—a position held
by such important officials as viziers or royal treasurers.
("Architect" is rather a free translation of this important
title; the office seems to have been a purely administrative
one, and there is little evidence that any of the men who held
it were practicing architects.) As further witness of the King's
confidence, Amunhotep was entrusted with the stewardship
of the estates of the Princess (later Queen) Sitamun, and he
was not only honored above all other men by being granted

the boon of a mortuary temple of his own in the sacred circle of the funerary temples of the kings, but was permitted to place sculptures of himself near those of his exalted master in the forecourt of the temple of Amun at Karnak. It is to the dedicatory inscriptions on his statues that we owe most of what we know about his career, though they reveal nothing of his character. Some indication of his renown and influence may be gained from an astonishing text on one of them, which offers his saintly intercession with Amun for him who stops to read.

During the last ten years of his reign, Amunhotep III showed great capriciousness of favor. If he mistrusted the ambitious Theban officials and the priests of Amun, he seems also to have mistrusted everybody else. Officials, one after another, experienced a meteoric rise and fall. Their disgrace is evident in the mutilations of their tombs; the reasons for it are never apparent. They may have furnished good grounds for royal suspicion by their intrigues. They may, on the other hand, have been victims of the whim of an ailing and crotchety ruler.

The son of Hapu was one of the few among Amunhotep's courtiers who retained his confidence to the end. He predeceased the King by a few years, but he left behind him in the post of vizier a kinsman named Ramose, who never fell from the Pharaoh's favor, and another relative, that Amunhotep who was Royal Steward at Memphis. The latter's son Ipi was one of the few representatives of established official families, Theban or Memphite, known to have followed Akhenaten to his new capital. With the Amarna revolution, most of the great families of the Eighteenth Dynasty disappeared into oblivion; but during the Ramesside period parvenu priests and officials, some of them of foreign ancestry, rigged for themselves false genealogies claiming descent from the men who had served the kings and the god Amun in Thebes at the height of its power.

CHAPTER FIVE

The Great Royal Wife—and Others

Shortly after his accession to the throne, Amunhotep III issued an announcement engraved on what are known to posterity as the "marriage scarabs." It reads quite simply:

> Long live King Amunhotep . . . and his Great Royal Wife Tiy. The name of her father is Yuya, the name of her mother is Tuya. She is the wife of a mighty King whose southern boundary is Karoy and whose northern boundary is Nahrin.

Since there is reason to believe that the marriage of Tiy and Amunhotep III may have been consummated while he was yet Crown Prince, these scarabs are not wedding announcements, but rather proclamations that the low-born Tiy, whose undistinguished parentage is clearly stated, is now empress of most of the known world. One can read an arrogance into the last sentence of the text, an assumption that a king whose power extends southward far into Nubia and to the northeastern confines of Syria can do as he pleases, regardless of precedent.

This scarab is not dated, but Tiy's name and queenly title appear on another commemorative scarab issued in the second year of Amunhotep's rule. Thenceforth, enclosed in a royal cartouche, it regularly accompanies that of the King, even in official statements of regnal years. It is joined with that of her lord in proclaiming that "miracle," the alliance of the Pharaoh with a princess of Mitanni. It appears side by side with that of Queen Sitamun, the daughter who grew up to share with her the title of Great Royal Wife. Over and over again in official sculptures and reliefs, Queen Tiy is shown enthroned beside the King.

The daughter of a provincial priest of Akhmim and a harem lady in the service of the King's mother, Tiy was accorded more prominence and honor than had been given to any previous queen. Her glory illuminated her obscure parents. Her father had titles heaped upon him, including the distinguished title of "God's Father," which frequently designated the fathers-in-law of rulers. Her mother became the chief lady of the harem of Amun. An uncle was made high priest at Heliopolis, and that Ay who served Amunhotep's son Akhenaten as Overseer of All the Horses of His Majesty and who acted as tutor and co-regent of Tutankhamun and briefly ruled as the last king of the Eighteenth Dynasty, is thought to have been her brother.

Yuya and Tuya were buried in the Valley of the Kings with almost royal pomp. The contents of their rich tomb, discovered by an American expedition a half-century past, were found almost intact. They included Yuya's chariot (for he was —or had become—Overseer of the King's Horses), as well as sumptuous gifts bearing the cartouche of Amunhotep III and fine inlaid and gold-encrusted furniture. On one chair the humble couple's royal granddaughter Sitamun is pictured as receiving "gold of the Southland."

It is hard to determine what qualities raised Tiy to her position in Amunhotep's far-from-stable affection and kept her there. Though she was not beautiful, her conventional-ized official portraits reveal a piquant charm. That charm is traceable in the features of an uninscribed wooden head, though there it is obscured by an expression that is not altogether pleasant. This head, formerly in Berlin, is thought by some to represent Tiy's daughter Sitamun. It portrays a queen with wide-set, slanting, heavy-lidded eyes, high forehead, rather prominent cheek bones, slightly protruding under lip, and sharp, determined chin. Though some of these features are evident, grossly exaggerated, in the portraits of Tiy's fanatical son Akhenaten, the head cannot be dismissed as a mere reflection of the "Amarna style": it is sufficiently like the earlier conventional representations of Tiy to suggest that it is a faithful portrait of a woman of determination and no little shrewdness. Whether it represents Tiy or the daughter who closely resembled her is a matter that must remain undecided.

The known facts concerning Tiy's career are relatively few. She was probably married, as was customary, at eleven or twelve years of age, became a widow at forty-eight or so, and died in her mid-sixties. She is known to have borne three daughters; she produced the successor to the throne, Akhenaten, only after many years of marriage. Her influence with her husband and the part she played in his counsels can be guessed from the prominence he accorded her throughout their entire life together and from a few references in the diplomatic correspondence preserved in the archives at Amarna. It was to her, as the widowed queen-mother, that the King of Mitanni appealed in the hope that she would use her influence with her son toward continuing the good relationship he had enjoyed with Egypt during the reign of Amunhotep III.

Some scholars have surmised that Tiy's was the intelligence inspiring Akhenaten's religious revolution. For that, there is no evidence. Like most kings, however, Akhenaten revered his mother, and she in turn continued to cherish her son. She paid a visit to him at Amarna, where he had built a residence for her. Whether she sojourned there and there died is not known. In any event, she apparently predeceased Akhenaten, happily unaware of the crumbling of his dream. In spite of her close association with him, she did not share in the obloquy attached to his name by future generations. She was remembered, not as the mother of the heretic, but as the Great Royal Wife of Amunhotep the Magnificent.

While Tiy had achieved a prouder position than that held by any former queen, the New Kingdom had been distinguished by a long series of remarkable royal ladies. When the defeat of the Hyksos was still only a dream in the minds of Theban kinglets of the late Seventeenth Dynasty, a young girl named Tetisheri—"Little Teti"—had come to Thebes as the wife of one of the petty rulers who defied the invaders with the claim that they were kings of Upper and Lower Egypt. Tetisheri is known to us through a hauntingly lovely sculptured portrait, but chiefly through the honors paid her by her grandson Ahmose, the conqueror of the Hyksos and the first king of the Eighteenth Dynasty, into whose reign she survived. Like Tiy, she was a commoner, and though the part she played in the Theban rise to power is uncertain, there seems little doubt that she had a share in the early struggle and later gave wise council to her illustrious grandson.

Her daughter Ahhotep, King Ahmose's mother, acted for a time practically as his co-regent. A stela erected by Ahmose to her during her lifetime stipulates that she be accorded substantially the same honors as given to himself. Its text credits her with having rallied troops and suppressed revolts, and presumably it was she who kept the home fires burning while Ahmose was engaged in the campaigns that led to the expulsion of the Hyksos and the triumph of the Theban Dynasty.

Ahhotep lived to see her grandson, Amunhotep I, on the throne; but long before she was buried in the Theban necropolis with the royal gifts Ahmose had heaped upon her, her place in the royal counsels had been usurped by her granddaughter Ahmose-Nofretari, Ahmose's niece and Great Royal Wife. This latter Queen, "great in favor" and "great in amiability," seems quite literally to have shared the throne of Egypt with her illustrious husband, who raised her to an hitherto unprecedented prominence. There has survived on a stela from her time a charmingly intimate record of the royal pair planning together a memorial to their common grandmother, Tetisheri. After Ahmose's death, Ahmose-Nofretari lived on as counselor to her son, Amunhotep I, who accorded her a place in his funerary temple and probably also in his tomb. As we have seen, she came to be worshiped with her son as a tutelary deity of the Theban necropolis, identified with Isis-Hathor, the prototype of royal motherhood.

The line of early Theban Great Royal Wives ended with Hatshepsut, the great-granddaughter of Tetisheri. She was not, as they had been, content to play a woman's part.

Women, especially as the mothers of men, had always enjoyed respect and honor in Egypt; but during the New Kingdom they acquired a new status, and this not only in royal circles. From early times the "lady of the house" had shared the life and fortunes of her husband and children in the close-knit family circle that was the basis of Egyptian society.

In a civilization innocent of surnames, a man identified himself as the "son of so-and-so." Sometimes he used the names of both parents, but not infrequently, forgetful of his paternity, he named only his mother. It was around the mother that the life of the household circled, and when her sons grew to manhood, she was not forgotten. A wise man of the New Kingdom echoed a common sentiment when he instructed his son to be mindful, when he had taken a wife and settled in his own house, of the mother who bore him.

> "Double the food of your mother and carry her as once she carried you. She had a heavy load in you. Even after your months were fulfilled, she still carried you clinging to her neck. For three years, her breast was in your mouth. She was not disgusted with your filth, nor did she say 'What can I do?' When you had been taught to write, she put you in school and each day brought you bread and beer from her store. Never let her raise her hands to God, crying out to Him of your neglect!"

As the wife was her husband's companion in life, so she was in death. While she was rarely granted a tomb of her own, she had her place in his tomb and shared his immortality. She was represented with him in funerary sculptures, though in the Old and Middle Kingdoms not always as quite his equal. Then she was shown with her arm about him in unreciprocated embrace or was pictured on a smaller scale than her mate, a few steps behind him or crouched at his side, clinging to his knee. Sculptures and pictured scenes of the New Kingdom seem to indicate that a wife was less subservient than she had been in earlier times. Statues—and there are more "pair statues" than ever before—represent man and wife in mutual embrace, and the paintings on tomb walls show them side by side as equals. From the Eighteenth Dynasty on, women become more and more boldly in evidence. The Greeks, who believed that the place of a respectable woman was in the gynaeceum, found the free manners of Egyptian females rather shocking.

As far back as anything is known about Egyptian society, it is apparent that kings and dignitaries had their harems, and during the opulence of the New Kingdom, more and more men could afford to increase their households with concubines and slaves. Even a relatively humble priest or official might boast at least one concubine; and while nothing is known concerning the relationship of men and women in the submerged classes, it is likely that among the peasantry some households included a concubine who doubled as an extra hand: as a modern Near Eastern proverb has it, "a woman comes cheaper than a donkey." There was no stigma attached to concubinage. Though a slave might serve as a concubine, a concubine was not a slave. It meant a step upward in the social scale for a family to place a daughter in the harem of a king or a great man. If she found favor in his eyes, she might be able to do something for her family; in any event, there would be one less mouth to feed. A girl brought up in a wealthy household, whether or not she had served as concubine to the master, frequently made a good marriage, and both she and her husband benefited from her former association. It seems to us almost a contradiction in terms to say that Egyptians were strictly monogamous. This, however, was the case. Relatively few kings had more than one Great Royal Wife, and still fewer commoners contracted more than a single marriage. In most families one woman and one alone held the honored title of "lady of the house." It was she who was recognized as the legal wife of her husband, and it was her sons who were his heirs.

"If thou be a man of standing," advises an ancient sage, "found a family and love thy wife as is fitting. Fill her belly, give her clothes for her back and ointment for her body, for she is a profitable field"—a field that will bear sons. A later moralist urges a little kindness to boot: "Act not the official over thy wife if she is diligent. Say not 'Where is it? Fetch it!' . . . Observe and be silent that thou mayst recognize her good deeds. It is thus that a man may avoid strife in his house."

Although marriage was a recognized and honored institution, we know little about the conditions or restrictions under which it was contracted. Women had legal rights practically equivalent to those of men; they could own or inherit or bequeath property and bring suit, but most of them probably had little to say about when or whom they would marry. A girl might become a wife at the age of eleven or twelve, a boy, a husband at about fourteen, so most marriages were a matter of arrangement between the bride's father and the prospective husband or his father. The bridegroom paid an agreed sum to the girl's father, and she in turn brought with her to her new home a dowry, usually in the form of goods and chattels.

Such conditions of marriage may be surmised for the Eighteenth Dynasty, though chiefly from late sources. Neither these sources nor any others give an inkling that marriage was celebrated with religious rites, nor is there the slightest evidence that nuptials were marked by special festivity; but it is hard to believe that the most religious of peoples could fail to invoke divine sanction of a marriage or that the festival-loving Egyptians could pass by so important an occasion for celebration as a wedding.

If there were prohibitory laws connected with marriage, few have come down to us. Contrary to the scandalous rumor that was probably set afloat by Diodorus and has persisted to this day, modern scholarship has found that brother-sister marriages in the pharaonic period were practically unknown among commoners, though close relationship such as that of uncle and niece or first cousins was no bar to matrimony. Men and women usually married within their own social class. While marriages with foreigners were not always favorably regarded, such alliances were not infrequent, nor were marriages between freemen and slaves. It has been assumed, on insufficient grounds, that legal marriage did not exist among the submerged classes, that with them, free unions were the rule. Though such may have been the case with unions between slaves, it is unlikely to have been true with freemen, especially if any property, however meager, or any inheritable right was involved.

Divorce was permissable for both men and women and apparently with little or no legal formality, but it seems to have been relatively rare. Since few women were economically independent, it was usually the husband who dissolved a marriage. Even incompatibility might be cause enough for him—he could send his wife home to her father in a fit of temper. In a letter written by a man to his dead wife, whose spirit he believed was haunting him, he apologizes: "I did the deed of a hasty man in repudiating thee." Sometimes (though the moralists discouraged this) a husband might wish to replace his wife with a younger and fairer woman or to contract another alliance, which would advance him in his career. And, finally, barrenness was a recognized cause for divorce, though even in that case we find at least one man and his wife agreeing to remain together and to make the children of a slave their legitimate heirs.

Adultery on the part of a married woman was the Great Sin, sometimes punishable by death. A man's committing adultery with another's wife was frowned upon. "Beware of approaching the woman of another house," counsels the wise Ptahhotep. "Don't be made a fool of by limbs of faïence. A bagatelle—a fleeting dream—knowing a strange woman is death." Another sage warns his son against a wife who is far from her husband; she is a "deep water, whose eddies are unknown."

While the over-all picture that emerges from the records is one of staid domesticity, with the polygamous instincts of the restless male taken care of by an accepted system of concubinage, there is some reason to believe that sexual morality did not always conform to standard. The student scribe is warned not only against drunkenness but against the loose women who haunted taverns. A man of the time of Amunhotep II, who became a High Priest of Amun in middle age, sententiously records his youthful deference to his father: he states piously that he was always obedient, never argumentative, listened to his parent with downcast eyes, and "knew not the handmaid of his house, lay not with his serving maid." Such negative evidence, together with indirect references to pederasty, offers some proof of an uncountenanced laxity such as has always existed in every place and every time.

In the New Kingdom there appears for the first time in history a literature of romantic love, a series of lyrics inscribed by Theban scribes of the Nineteenth and Twentieth Dynasties, sometimes on the backs of official documents. Though none of these manuscripts dates from the period of Amunhotep III, there is reason to believe that these or similar songs were sung by the light-hearted people of his court. Perhaps there had always been love songs handed down among the folk, but if so, they had never before been put into writing. The nearest approach to love lyrics in the written literature of earlier times is found in hymns to Hathor, solemn and impersonal. Now, with the new luxury and freedom of manners, there blossoms a whole new poetry in praise of love, a bit artificial, but as delicately lovely as any that has ever been written. Made to be sung to lute or lyre, the melody of the songs escapes us, along with the music of their accompaniment, but their themes are universal—the pleasures of love, the agony of separation, the joy of reunion; and their voluptuousness is innocent. The songs contain almost no allusions to religion or magic, strangely little that appears to us today as remote or foreign. On the contrary, these earliest of all romantic love songs have a familiar ring; their themes have long since become hackneyed.

Perhaps no better conclusion to a chapter on the position of women in the Eighteenth Dynasty can be found than a free paraphrase of a few of the lyrics. The graceful verses do not hold the answer to any of the problems concerning the relationship of the sexes that have been raised in these pages, but they can hardly fail to lend warmth and color to a picture of life in Thebes during the affluence of the New Kingdom.

When I kiss her parted lips
I am happy—even without beer.

The Great Royal Wife—and Others

I wish I were the negress, her handmaiden!
I wish I were the washerman who rinses the sweet ointment
from her garments!
I wish I were the ring she wears on her finger!

How sweet to bathe in your presence!
In the water my dress of royal linen
Clings wet, so that you may see my beauty.
When I go with you to the lake
I bring you a red fish that lies fair on my fingers.
Come look at me!

I wish I were your housewife—
I wish your arm might be twined with mine!
If you do not come tonight
I shall be like one dead and laid in her grave
Are you not my health and my life?

I came in the darkness,
I knocked and no one answered....
The choicest bits of our ox
Are for the carpenter-boy
Who will make a bolt of reed,
A door of straw,
So that I may come at will
To find the house open,
And a bed spread with fine linen,
And a fair maid beside it.

Your love awaits me across the river.
A crocodile lies on the sandbar,
But I go boldly into the water—
The waves are land under my feet.
It is your love that makes me strong;
It weaves a water-spell for me.

Thebes

When I see you coming
My heart dances;
My arms open wide to hold you.

Seven days it is from yesterday
That I have not seen her!
A sickness has crept over me. . . .
The physicians come
But my heart finds no comfort in their potions.
The magicians are without resource.
No one knows the cause of my malady.
Only she can raise me up,
Only her messengers can give strength to my heart.
When I see her, then I am well.
When she looks at me my limbs are young again,
When I hold her in my arms evil takes wing.
But she has gone from me these seven days.

I am your first beloved,
A garden planted with flowers and sweet herbs. . . .
How beautiful the place where we walk, hand in hand!
I am happy because we walk together.
The sound of your voice is sweet—
I live when I hear it.
The sight of you is food and drink to me.

(Adapted from A. Erman, *The Literature of the Ancient Egyptians* . . . , tr. by A. M. Blackman [London, 1927], and A. H. Gardiner, *The Chester Beatty Papyri No. I* [Oxford, 1931].)

CHAPTER SIX

The Divine Order

Amunhotep III may well have believed in the mystery of his birth as he had it depicted on the walls of the temple he built at Luxor. As Crown Prince, he was probably told that fable in the nursery, and certainly no doubter in his entourage ever dared to hint that it was false. Most of his people believed in it. If, as the son of a god, he yet proudly claimed descent from a long line of human rulers and, like any good son, paid filial respect to the dead king who had been his earthly father, such trifling inconsistencies bothered nobody.

The concept of god-king was a religious one, and religion is a matter of faith, not of logic. It was no harder for an Egyptian to believe in the miraculous conception of his ruler, his consequent divinity, and his ultimate apotheosis than it is for a modern Christian to believe in the Virgin Birth, the Word Made Flesh, and the Resurrection of Christ. Though his courtiers praised the king in extravagant terms as all-powerful and all-seeing, it was evident to everybody, including himself, that he was neither omniscient nor omnipotent. He had to have his officials to be, as they boasted, "eyes and ears" for him. Although divine himself, he nevertheless found it necessary to appeal to the gods in times of stress; in fortune he gave thanks to the gods. He was pictured on the walls of temples as an equal in the company of deities, but also as a worshiper and suppliant. He brought offerings and poured libations to the gods; he knelt, even prostrated himself, before them. His human limitations were obvious. He could be flattered and fooled; he could suffer sickness and die. But so could the immortal gods. They, too, could be cajoled and hoodwinked and cheated by men; they had foes from whom they had to be protected with prophylactic rites; they sometimes experienced pain and the temporary eclipse of death. The folk knew all these things. They spun irreverant tales about kings and converted myths of the gods into rollicking, earthy stories, and the essential divinity of rulers and deities remained unaltered.

Upon the king, upholder of Maat, depended the order of the world as established at the moment of creation. He was the appointed and only recognized mediator between the gods and his people. His responsibility entailed a moral obligation; he was expected to act in accordance with truth ("revealed" truth) and justice. Theology made a subtle distinction between the reigning pharaoh and his divinely established office, between the king as a man and as the vessel of the god, between the living, human ruler and the deified dead one. Such fine distinctions were beyond the grasp of most people. There were good kings and bad kings—that everybody recognized. The folk embalmed their rancor against the oppression of the pyramid builders, for instance, in tales still current at the time of Herodotos; but with the (to us apparent) illogicality inherent in Egyptian thought, the masses could accept the humanity of a ruler and still regard him as a god. Kings were plotted against, in rare cases deposed, even assassinated, but never (this Frankfort has pointed out) as a result of popular uprising.

Instances can be cited to show that Amunhotep III, like

most kings, understood the human limitations of his power. On a stela he erected at Abydos, his circumscribed function is neatly expressed in a hymn addressed to Amun by a divine chorus: "Thou art in heaven and thou shinest for the earth, while he [the King] is on earth exercising thy kingship." But there are other indications that Amunhotep may, in his arrogance, have considered himself nothing short of divine. History offers no evidence that he was exceptionally intelligent. His blind egotism makes itself felt in his every utterance, his every deed. Though no Egyptian pharaoh had ever been reticent about his own merits, Amunhotep outdid his predecessors in boasting, in the size and number of statues of himself he erected in temples consecrated to the gods. Former kings had not expected consummation of divinity until after death; only then were the rites due to gods performed for them. Amunhotep III established his cult while he was still alive, sharing honors with Amun in the funerary temple which he built on the West Bank at Thebes and with Ptah at the sanctuary he constructed at Memphis. At Sulb he is pictured not merely as consorting with the gods, but as embracing and bringing offerings to his own divine self in the temple called "Shining-in-Maat," which he built as a monument for his own image, and where he called himself "Lord of Nubia," and also "Great God, Lord of Heaven."

Some scholars see in Amunhotep's self-aggrandizement only a propagandist effort made to counteract the growing influence of the priesthood of Amun. Upstart rulers of the past had, it is true, found it necessary to claim descent falsely from earthly rulers or to stress their divine parentage, but Amunhotep came from a long-established line of god-descended kings; and there is little evidence that he feared the Theban priesthood or doubted his power to control it. His insistence on his miraculous birth and his right as a living king to divine honors may well have been an assertion of his own belief. He was a man of his time.

In our day, if (as sometimes happens) a man claims to be the chosen instrument of God, he is looked upon as a charlatan or, at best, somewhat unbalanced. If he claims to be God, he is adjudged insane. It is difficult for us to see the past except in the light of our own accumulated knowledge, our own faith or lack of faith. However impartial we may try to be, it is all but impossible for us to enter into the mentality of a people remote from us in time and experience. Though religious concepts similar to those of the ancient Egyptians have persisted down to our own time among peoples of Asia and Africa, it remains difficult for us, misled by the extraordinarily advanced accomplishments of the Egyptians in organization and administration, their inventiveness and skill, to grasp the essential archaism of their mentality, to imagine them as actuated by convictions much different from our own or to realize the extent to which religion permeated their life and thought. Thus, though Egyptian religion is a subject that defies brief analysis—indeed, almost any analysis at all— some idea of the beliefs current in Thebes must unavoidably be given in an account of a city whose history is so inextricably intertwined with the faith of its rulers and their people.

In very rough outline, it may be said of the Thebans, as of all other Egyptians, that they possessed, underlying a surface of accumulated myth and formalistic and magical practice, three fundamental and, in essence, universal religious ideas: a belief, however vague and diffused, in a supreme god, creator of all things; a belief in a divine order established at the moment of creation, with the kingship as the earthly vehicle of that order; above all, a belief in life after death.

In a land of almost unvarying sunshine, fertilized by a nearly always dependable annual flood, it was easy to believe in a Power that had created an unchanging and unchangeable universe and an order that would endure forever unaltered. Such a belief is common to many religions, including some of the greatest among them. Extended as it was by the Egyptians, however, from the metaphysical into the temporal realm of government and economics, it was not (as John Wilson has remarked) a faith that made for progress, that provided for man's unceasing readjustment to a fundamentally changeless but, on the surface, ever-changing universe. It may have comfortably relieved him of responsibility for his fate, but it kept him enslaved to his own puny past.

The concept of a universal god, creator of all things, had its origin in the earliest times. The creator had many aspects, and many places laid claim to being the site of creation, most frequently a primeval hill rising out of the dark waters of chaos like a mound emerging from the receding flood of the Nile; but even before history an idea of beginning in which the life-giving sun played the leading role began to percolate the land.

In dim antiquity, when men first banded together, each group or clan had raised up its god, a god usually manifest in an animal, a plant, a stone, or a fetish, very rarely until historic times in human form. Predominant were the animal gods, worshiped for their fecundity or virility, their strength, their terribleness. Some of the many primitive deities signified, or came to signify, cosmic phenomena, earth and air, wind and water, the ever departing and ever returning astral bodies. Some, from their names, seem to have come to represent the ineffability of deity—"The Distant," "The Hidden," "The Complete."

As time went on, the primitive clans were gathered by conquest or for convenience into associations, and Egypt was gradually divided into what were later to become provinces or (as the Greeks called them) nomes. In the beginning, these were independent petty kingdoms, each with its own ruler and its own god, the god of the most powerful group in the association. Since each of the clans composing a nome clung to its own ancestral god, additional deities were given place in the hierarchy of the chief god as his attributes or associates. Thus a nome god usually acquired a family consisting of a wife (or husband) and child. That the triads formed in this and other manners were frequently by nature incompatible apparently interfered not at all with divine domesticity.

Although the boundaries of the nomes shifted in historic times and original units were combined or divided, the identity of many of the primitive associations was never lost; down into Roman times some of the nomes retained their ancient names and age-old standards, which bore aloft primeval deities or their symbols. For many Egyptians, unschooled in theology, their regional god always remained pre-eminent; but even before history, religious ideas of certain more advanced and politically more powerful centers began to filter through the country, and a number of deities personifying cosmic forces or more or less abstract ideas came to receive widespread, if not universal, veneration.

With the passing centuries there came into being larger federations composed of several loosely united nomes. Shortly before history, these larger federations seem at times to have consisted of two imperfectly amalgamated groups, one in Lower Egypt and one in Upper Egypt. There is even a possibility that the Two Lands may have enjoyed a brief coalition under a single ruler before the final unification took place. However that may be, it was in the early federations that the Egyptian administrative genius had its birth; certainly an irrigation system, impossible without some measure of large-scale co-operation, had been initiated, peaceful trade had paved the way for a homogeneous way of life throughout the land, and the traders, as so often, had carried with them religious ideas that came to find common acceptance.

It is often wondered how Egypt could appear in history so fully panoplied in wisdom. Her sudden burgeoning at the beginning of the dynastic period in arts and skills, in capacity for rule, in theological speculation, and, above all, the miraculous speed with which she learned to express herself in writing have been explained variously as due to the advent of a "new race" or, at the very least, to knowledge passed on from older civilizations of the Near East. Some inspiration from the East there certainly was, though it was mainly on the surface; that it was brought by a "new race" is now doubted. The fact remains that Egypt was in many ways strangely matured before she emerged into history, and her civilization was, in the truest sense, autochthonous.

Not long after the first historic kings of the Two Lands established themselves at Memphis, they adopted Ptah, an anthropomorphic deity they found there, as creator of gods and men and founder of the divine order. The myth of creation, which was copied on enduring stone in the Late Period, seems from internal evidence to have been formulated, at least in part, at a time about the beginning of the Pyramid Age, although many of its concepts may have had their origin in prehistory. In the Memphite theology, Ptah is not only the creator of gods and men but also, as Ta-Tenen, the primeval hill. He is the giver of being to Atum, established as creator at Heliopolis, and to Osiris, the resurrected and deified king who came to represent the Egyptians' hope for immortality. However obfuscated by myth and allusion, the Memphite theology has grandeur. While what we know of most other Egyptian theologies seems to make of creation a physical act on the part of creator or demiurge, the system recorded by the Memphite priests is inspired by the idea of a divine intelligence. It represents the universe as conceived in the heart of Ptah and brought into being by his utterance. "In the beginning was the Word and the Word was with God and the Word was God. All things were made through Him."

Although Ptah came to be revered throughout Egypt as one of the great gods, he was always primarily a Memphite, the god of the ancient capital and the dynasties that had held sway there. He was venerated elsewhere not chiefly (except perhaps among theologians) in his capacity of creator of the universe, but in that of artificer. It was he, the Memphite theology unfolds, who fashioned the "bodies" of the gods, "of every wood, of every stone, of every clay," for them to inhabit in the world of men; and thus Ptah became the archetype and patron of artists and craftsmen.

Of greater influence than Memphis in Egyptian religious life was the older city, Heliopolis, in which was developed the solar cult that eventually dominated the land. Never politically pre-eminent in historic times, Heliopolis was yet the spiritual heart of Egypt. It gave of its gods to the Memphite kings and drew Memphite gods into its circle; it inspired the dogma of Thebes; it paved the way for Akhenaten's crusade to establish the visible disk of the sun as sole god. Until its destruction, Heliopolis was a holy place, repository for the wisdom of the past.

In that hoary city, Atum was the creator, the All from which all issued. He was associated with the scarab beetle, which the Egyptians thought to be, as the god himself had been, self-generating. The name given to the beetle signified "to come into being," "to become," and the scarab passed down the centuries, not only as an amulet, potent with ever renewing life, but as an aspect and avatar of the creator. Though Atum was early succeeded by the sun god Re, he was never eclipsed by him. He remained the All, with Re as the demiurge. It was both Re and Atum-Re whose light illumined the world.

Just when the Heliopolitan solar religion was crystallized into a theology is uncertain. It had its roots in prehistory; it seeps through the Pyramid Texts; it inspired the pyramids themselves; but it became paramount in the Fifth Dynasty. Earlier kings of united Egypt had contented themselves chiefly with raising grandiose tombs for their own occupancy and only modest domiciles for the gods, but the rulers of the Fifth Dynasty, frequently assuming names compounded with that of Re, whose sons they claimed to be, erected magnificent temples to the sun god and expropriated vast territories for their endowment. What with the lands assigned for the building and maintenance of the tombs of kings and courtiers and those taken over for the earthly sustenance of the royal household and an ever increasing circle of officials, all directly or indirectly fed from the "table of the king," private owner-ship of land gradually became almost nonexistent; the masses were reduced to tenancy and serfdom.

In the open courts that formed the sanctuaries of the sun temples of the Fifth Dynasty, there appeared squat monu-ments crowned with gilded pyramidions that caught the rays of the rising sun. These structures imitated the *benben* stone of Heliopolis, situated on the primeval hill, to which at each dawning Re sent his beams in a re-enactment of the miracle of creation. From these monuments, and indirectly from the primitive stone that had been venerated from time immemo-rial, sprang the great obelisks that towered over Thebes.

From Hierakonpolis far up the Nile, the earliest kings of Egypt had brought with them to Memphis another solar divinity, the falcon Horus, whose eyes were the sun and the moon and whose wings spanned the firmament. Perhaps originally a Lower Egyptian divinity, Horus became simul-taneously synonomous with the immortal sun and the living god-king. The first rulers of united Egypt called themselves "Horus," and pharaohs retained a Horus-name in their tit-ularies forever after. Horus was early drawn into the Helio-politan circle of Re, and from the Fifth Dynasty on, rulers saw no incongruity in calling themselves at once the sun (Horus) and sons of the sun (Re).

At about the same time, Horus emerges in a new capacity as the son of Osiris, the god who was to mean more to Egyp-tians of future ages than any other, for he represented their hope for eternal life. Osiris, who had long been revered in the Delta, was thought to have once lived on earth as a mortal ruler; and there is a vague possibility that he may actually have been a king or chieftain in a forgotten past. The story goes that he was a good and wise king who ruled over all Egypt, teaching his people husbandry, establishing laws to guide them, and instructing them in the respect and homage due the gods. He was murdered by his jealous brother Seth (an Upper Egyptian deity of the mysterious western wastes and their far-flung oases, represented as a doglike animal of undetermined species and terrifying character), who threw his body into the Nile. Horus undertook to avenge his father and establish his own right to the succession, and after a long fight, he triumphed over his wicked uncle to inherit the throne of the Two Lands.

The epic contest of Horus and Seth, here so baldly stated, emerges in scraps from a number of documents; but it survives most completely in a lusty, irreverent folk tale, written in the racy vernacular of the Nineteenth Dynasty. Some hold that the myth symbolizes a struggle between light and darkness, good and evil, common to the thought and mythologies of many peoples; but other modern scholars see in it a dimly remembered episode in the long fight for the mastery of Egypt, when the North (Horus) had temporarily vanquished the South (Seth), which, in the end, having captured Horus for its own, was to prove victorious.

The story of Osiris does not end with his death. The murdered king had early been identified, probably at Busiris in the Delta, with an ancient god of vegetation; and as plants grow and die and are reborn, so it was told that Osiris died and was buried and rose from the dead. In the tale of his resurrection, the goddess Isis, who apparently originally personified the royal throne, appears as his wife. Aided by a posthumously born Horus, she rescues the body of her husband, which the formidable Seth had dismembered and scattered far and wide, to have it joined together and magically resuscitated by Atum-Re, the creator. The risen king was given a place among the gods as ruler of the Underworld; Isis became the archetype of wifehood and motherhood; and the child Horus became the personification not only of the inherited right of kings, but of filial piety in general.

The cult of Isis endured down the ages, increasing in extent and fervor as the ancient civilization neared its close. The archaism of late times occasionally represented the goddess by a throne; sometimes she was shown as a throne-crowned woman; but more often she wore the horns and disk of the cow-eared Hathor, mother-goddess and goddess of love, with whom she came to be merged. Countless figures of Isis holding the holy child in her arms were manufactured to be offered as ex-votos or to be set up on household altars as objects of personal devotion. Her mysteries were celebrated throughout the Roman world; her shaven priests appeared in far-off Albion.

As Horus became the personification of the living king, so Osiris personified the dead king, who was united with him after death to share in his immortality. In the beginning, only the pharaoh could hope for such mystic union, but gradually the privilege was extended to the royal family and then to others in the entourage of the ruler. Little by little, the circle widened, until even the humblest could aspire to becoming an Osiris, resurrected to life everlasting.

In the troubled times of the First Intermediate Period, there developed an earlier idea that a future life might in some measure depend upon a person's righteousness in the world of the living, and Osiris came to be looked upon not only as ruler but as judge of the dead. Moral precepts handed down from the Old Kingdom show that there had always existed in Egypt a standard of ethics, but it was an ethics based primarily on expediency and decency, on getting on in the world and along with one's fellow men. Only rarely did it express the idea that uprightness might be pleasing to God.

The connection between religion and ethics remained tenuous. Illuminated funerary papyri of the New Kingdom found at Thebes picture the deceased before the awesome tribunal of the Underworld, where his heart is being weighed in the balance against a feather, the attribute of the goddess Maat, who represented truth and justice, righteousness, and above all, the established order. Such papyri frequently contain what is known to modern scholars as the "negative confession," in which the deceased claims not to have committed any of a long and repetitious list of sins. Most of the perennial sins forbidden by the Ten Commandments are included, as well as others not explicitly stated in that all-time rule for decent conduct. The defendant at the court of Osiris avows, for instance, that he has not indulged in pederasty, that he has not falsified his taxes nor taken more than his just share of irrigation waters, that he has not failed in respect toward his betters nor in loyalty to the king, that he has not neglected the ritual observance due the gods. Even here a truly religious idea is not paramount. In the judgment, as in other trials along the road to bliss, the deceased had the aid of magic. Like the demons and monsters who beset him on his way, the eternal gods, too, could be hoodwinked by spells and incantations. The negative confession is itself a spell rather than a contrite avowal; and a potent chapter of the Book of the Dead conjures man's heart to silence, lest it testify against him at the judgment seat.

Although the fundamental religious concepts as outlined early in this chapter were generally accepted throughout Egypt, the country never knew a single, unified religion. Belief remained fluid, never crystallized into dogma. Successive dynasties raised to eminence this god or that as dynastic patron, but no king ever sought to impose his deity by force on the people as a whole. Different theologies existed side by side without rivalry, freely exchanging ideas, divinities, and ritual practices. There were no acrimonious disputes of theologians, no bloody wars between sects, no proselytism, no intolerance, save in the brief period during which Akhenaten tried to institute a much-needed religious reform and in the time immediately following his unsuccessful attempt.

It is not surprising that the Theban theology as formulated in the course of the Eighteenth Dynasty should have borrowed from the theologies of Memphis and Heliopolis (presented above in an oversimplified and superficial manner, with hardly any indication of their scholastic involutions or their political significance), and from the theologies of lesser centers as well. It accumulated, but it added little or nothing that was new. As the great Erman said a hundred years ago, the curse of the Egyptians was that they could never forget. An ancient sage who made a blessing of this curse—"Every word [of the ancestors] is carried on forever in this land, without perishing"—spoke only too truly. Few of the conflicting concepts formed during the infancy of the race were ever entirely discarded; few deities passed into oblivion; and new gods were added from time to time to a pantheon whose members combined and exchanged attributes and functions to a point of inextricable confusion. Confusion it was to Egyptian theologians who on occasion tried, with marked lack of success, to bring order out of chaos; confusion it is to modern scholars who endeavor to extract meaning from religious texts, the majority of which were compiled in antiquity from miscellaneous sources that were frequently already archaic and only vaguely understood (when at all) by the scribes who employed them.

It is easy for us to see why Egyptian religion, which lasted for more than three thousand years, never became a universal spiritual force nor produced a valid and coherent philosophy of life. Yet there were some Egyptians who caught a glimpse of the sublime beyond the multitudinous deities, the frozen ritual, the desperate attempt at foiling fate by magical practices. As early as the Old Kingdom, a few men could reveal in their writings a conception, not of a god or gods, but of God in the abstract, and of man's need through God to make his peace with the world. "It is not the intentions of men that are fulfilled, but the plan of God" (Man proposes, but God disposes!) writes Ptahhotep. "God knows him who acts for him," says Akhtoy to his son. "He knows every [man by] name." Many similar phrases, some of which anticipate the wisdom of the Old Testament, are interspersed through the hardheaded worldliness of Egyptian moral literature: "God wishes of thee respect for the poor more than honor to the great"; "God hates him who speaks falsely"; "Happy is he who walks in the way of God." The confusing syncretism practiced by the Egyptians is itself a reaching after a universal god—a tendency to make of the many, manifestations of the one. And indeed, regardless of local differences in attributes or functions, Egyptian deities follow a strikingly similar pattern and show an essential oneness.

In Thebes the drama of Creation unfolded in much the

same way as it had elsewhere, with a change only in setting and dramatis personae. Amun became the creator and Thebes the site of the primeval hill. Some think that Amun was originally one of the primitive gods of Hermopolis, the city that had apparently once been a rival of Heliopolis. In Hermopolis an Amun, "The Hidden One," was a god of the atmosphere, who seems to have signified, or to have come to signify, the breath that animates all living things. Many scholars suspect, however, largely for etymological reasons, that Amun may have been a local Theban god of similar name and unknown antecedents, who took over some of the characteristics of the Hermopolitan deity, as he did those of Min, a fertility god of nearby Koptos. Amun's connection with Min is indisputable. He was frequently called Min-Amun, and his earliest known representations show him in the guise of his ithyphallic neighbor.

Amun was, however, a protean god, who adopted many forms. Sometimes he appeared as a ram, sometimes as a goose. More rarely he manifested himself in what may have been his original aspect, a primeval serpent, living in Djeme, the "Most Sacred Place of Amun" (now Medinet Habu), in a chthonian cave. Commonly Amun took human form, crowned as a king, his crown borrowing the twin feathers of Min, the twisted horns of the virile ram, the sun disk and uraeus of Re, or all three attributes.

He was worshiped not only in the Nile Valley. He had his sanctuaries in Nubia and the East, for his rays reached the ends of the earth. In his homeland, though his wealth and influence ultimately dwindled, he was never forgotten. In the vassal countries of Asia, his worship declined with Egypt's power; there, Isis-Hathor and the child Horus lingered in popular imagination longest of any of the Egyptian divinities. But centuries after the empire ceased to be, when Egypt was ruled by alien kings and the temple of Karnak was little more than a shabby ruin, the cult of Amun was fiercely cherished by half-savage petty kings of Nubia.

The emergence of Amun in the Eleventh Dynasty and his rise to prominence in the Twelfth have here been previously indicated. While some of the rulers of the Middle Kingdom declared "Amun-Is-Foremost" in the names they took, they gave him only a share of their devotion. To the rulers of the Eighteenth Dynasty he was foremost in very truth. It was he who had established the dynasty, given victory to its kings, and brought prosperity to the land. It was not for political reasons alone that the kings built temples for him and endowed them with lands and slaves and captured wealth. They believed in him. By showering riches upon him, they hoped to ensure his continued support for themselves and their people. It was not solely to fortify their own hold on Egypt that they made him king of the gods, bringing all other gods and their temples and priesthoods under his control. Though they may have had, consciously or subconsciously, an *arrière-pensée,* the fact remains that they believed, they and their subjects.

Thebans knew little or nothing of the devious history of their religion, which modern scholars have tried to trace; they accepted the multiple gods, the confusion of religious ideas handed down to them, with unquestioning faith. It was natural (if they thought about it at all) that the all-conquering Amun should have absorbed the ancient Re; natural, too, to worship Amun-Re and to continue to venerate both gods as separate entities or in other combinations. There was nothing strange in the fact that Ptah should have been drawn into the Theban circle by the theologians to form a mystical trinity with Amun and Re, or that other great and lesser deities should have gravitated to the court of the king of the gods at Karnak.

These deities, though subordinated to the supreme god, retained their identities. Many gods became specialists, each to be appealed to in his own line. It has already been noted that Montu, who had led the royal ancestors of the Eleventh Dynasty to victory, still retained an eminence as a god of battles. Sometimes, as Montu-Re, he shared with Amun the honor of assimilation with the sun god. Though his chief residence was in the neighboring town of Armant, the capital of the Theban nome before the rise of The City, he had an ancient shrine also in the Theban suburb of Medamud, and Amunhotep III built for him a temple of surpassing splendor within the precincts of Karnak.

Khnum, creator ram god, the divine potter who modeled mankind on his turning wheel, was pictured on the walls of Luxor temple as fashioning the future Amunhotep III. He had perhaps been brought to Thebes from Elephantine by the hardy adventurers of that border city, who had long served the pharaohs well as leaders of desert expeditions and as intrepid explorers and sailors. As Khnum-Amun, the ram god was merged with the Lord of Thebes.

In a city of clerks, it was natural that Thoth should be honored. He was "Great in Magic," inventor of language and writing, custodian of all learning. He was the tongue of Ptah, which by its utterance brought the universe into being, but was also creator in his own right; in his aspect of ibis, he was believed to have laid on the primeval hill at his city,

Hermopolis, the cosmic egg from which the sun was born. Probably rather early in his long career, he was or became a moon god, the "Re-Who-Shines-by-Night." As such he was frequently represented as a cynocephalous ape or a man, moon crowned; and since the earliest Egyptian calendar was a lunar one, he was revered as the reckoner of time, the length of kings' reigns, and men's days. He was the patron of physicians, who mixed magic with their medicines, as well as of scribes. Many a Theban office was presided over by the image of an ape, and many a clerk had himself represented in adoration before the god in his bird or animal form. As scribe of the gods, it was Thoth who held the balance at the judgment of the dead.

Although no shrine of Osiris is known in Thebes of the New Kingdom, where Amun held sway also over the necropolis, the King of the Dead was nevertheless omnipresent in royal and private funerary beliefs and rites. The divine mother Isis and the child Horus were venerated by great and small. Since each king was a "living Horus," the god was closely connected with the cult of the kingship; as avenger and successor of his father Osiris, he was not only the archetype of filial piety but also the personification of the royal right of succession. The importance of Horus grew with the increasing influence of the Heliopolitan solar cult, in which he was venerated as Re-Herakhte, the sun at its rising.

Very little is heard of Seth during the late Eighteenth Dynasty in his homeland of Upper Egypt. Kings sometimes called themselves both Horus and Seth in token of their rule over both lands, and in myth the turbulent deity had partially vindicated himself by protecting the sun-god from the daily attacks of the devouring serpent Apophis; but the cult of Seth was now confined chiefly to the Delta. There, it will be re-membered, the Hyksos had adopted him; and though this may not have greatly added to his credit with the Thebans, it was not until toward the end of the pharaonic period that he came to be regarded with abhorrence as a personification of evil. The Ramessides, forsaking Thebes for a capital in the Delta, adopted Seth as their dynastic god, though they still vowed their allegiance—and their wealth—to Amun.

Thebes knew many Hathors. In fact, Hathor appears with such chameleonlike changes that her name sometimes seems to signify hardly more than a generic term for "goddess." The people related the myth of how, as the eye of Re, Hathor was sent to destroy mankind, whose evil ways had become anathema to the sun god. In the midst of the carnage, Re repented of his wrath but managed to restrain the ravaging goddess only by making her drunk with reddened beer, offered to her in lieu of blood. Most Thebans, however, thought of Hathor as a kindly goddess of love and mirth and music—the goddess of near-by Denderah, whose feast was celebrated with singing and dancing and pleasant drunken-ness in the streets of Thebes and throughout Egypt. Hathor was usually represented as a woman with a cow's head or with human head and cow's ears and horns, and she undoubtedly combined in her person a number of sacred cows that had been worshiped in scattered places from remote times. At a shrine in the necropolis near Deir el Bahri (perhaps on a site made holy by an earlier, forgotten cow goddess), she nourished the ruler, the "living Horus," and as patroness of the necropolis protected him and his people in death as in life. In Theban tombs she sometimes appeared as a tree spirit, "Goddess of the Sycamore," to pour out life-giving water for the dead from her leafy abode. And finally, seven Hathors presided like fairies at the birth of an Egyptian child, bestowing on him the gifts allotted to him by fate.

Among all these divinities and many others the Theban kings and their people distributed their offerings and homage. Even foreign gods were hospitably received. This was to be expected in a cosmopolitan age such as that of the New Kingdom, and acquaintance with the ideas and ideals of a larger world may well have helped the fermentation of the religious revolution that was already brewing in the time of Amunhotep III. Yet, even in his day, familiar as they had become, foreigners were on the whole looked down upon—only Egyptians were called men.

Few Egyptians were adventurers. Voyages to other lands were usually undertaken fearfully and unwillingly; sojourn in a strange country was in the nature of exile, and death and burial there the most tragic of fates. At home, however, Egyptians were indefatigable travelers. Men who held or administered widely scattered estates voyaged often and far to look after their own interests or those of king or overlord. Officials and minor servants of the highly centralized government made frequent trips for supervision of local authorities or traveled hither and yon on royal missions. The royal family, attended by vast retinues, moved from palace to palace, according to whim or season. Above all, everybody who could went on pilgrimages.

There was no lack of holy places to provide Thebans with excuse for a trip, no lack of religious festivals offering food and drink and entertainment; but one of the chief centers of pilgrimage was Abydos, the burial place of Osiris. Though a number of other sanctuaries, including one at Memphis, claimed the body of the god, or at least a part of it, Abydos was the chief among them and perhaps the oldest. It seems natural that Osiris, the personification of the dead king, should have been thought by the Egyptians to rest in the cemetery where the earliest rulers of united Egypt had been buried. In the necropolis at Abydos, the King of the Dead held sway as creator on his own primeval hill, surrounded by a court of canine deities. He absorbed a local dog-god, Khentamenty, who had preceded him at the site as "Lord of the West (the cemetery)," and he drew into his circle Wapwawet, a primitive watchdog of Asyut, as well as the jackal Anubis, who had come from the Delta city near Busiris that the Greeks called "Dogtown" to become patron of embalmers and guardian of cemeteries throughout the land.

While rulers of the Pyramid Age and later were buried at Memphis, they provided themselves with Nile boats for an imaginary voyage to Abydos and erected cenotaphs near the tomb of the god with whom they expected to be united in death. During the troubled times that followed the Old Kingdom, especially during the bitter struggle between the Herakleopolitans and the Thebans, the holy ground was fought over, its tombs and cenotaphs sacked and destroyed. The kings of the Eleventh Dynasty did only a little to reclaim the cemetery, but Twelfth Dynasty pharaohs undertook its revival; and it is during their rule that one first hears of the passion play dramatizing episodes from the myth of Osiris, which was performed each year at Abydos just before the crops sprang to new life from the black earth.

In the New Kingdom, Abydos could justly claim the title of "Second Heliopolis" (which it shared, incidentally, with a number of other places, including Thebes), for it completely eclipsed the Heliopolis of the North as a place of pilgrimage. At the beginning of the period, a natural mound in the necropolis was shown to the faithful as the tomb of the god, but during the rule of Amunhotep III, in what was perhaps the first archaeological excavation on record, the tomb of King Djer of the First Dynasty was uncovered and identified as the holy sepulcher. In the uneasy days of their rise to power, the first kings of the Eighteenth Dynasty had taken thought to build cenotaphs in the sacred cemetery. Already in the Twelfth Dynasty, Egyptians had aspired to burial near the tomb of Osiris. As time passed, more and more persons arranged for interment at Abydos or erected there mock tombs or stelae to serve as burials by proxy. Many others had the voyage to Abydos pictured on the walls of their tombs in Thebes or elsewhere as a magical substitute for a final pilgrimage, at the end of which they hoped to share in the immortality of the god and the offerings given him for sustaining life eternal.

Just what form that life would take was a hazy enough matter. Egyptians held conflicting views on the subject, inherited from their long past. One might become Re in his bark, journeying across the heavens by day and illuminating the gloom of the underworld by night. At the same time, one might become Osiris or, simultaneously, one of his subjects. Again, one might join a royal galaxy as a star of the firmament. But, after all, it was perfectly possible that one might continue to live in his tomb, enjoying the good things of this world there provided for him and at times issuing forth in one guise or another to breathe the air and look upon the fair land of Egypt. It was toward a continued existence in their tombs that most Egyptians leaned.

In a beautifully illuminated copy of the Book of the Dead taken with him on his journey into the unknown by a Theban of the New Kingdom named Ani, he is shown with his wife, happily working in the Blessed Fields of the hereafter, harvesting a miraculous wheat with stalks six feet tall and fat ears twenty inches in length. Since Ani and his wife were of a class unaccustomed to toil, this pictured scene represents only a pretty fancy; they had undoubtedly provided themselves with a goodly number of ushabtis, mummiform figures in their own likeness which would serve as magical substitutes for them in case they should be called upon to tend the irrigation ditches or till the soil of Eternity.

In the same papyrus, Ani anxiously inquires of the god Atum what the "silent land" to which he is bound is like, and Atum replies: "It has no water, it has no air. Deep, deep—dark, dark—boundless, boundless . . . Sexual love is not enjoyed there. But transfigured being is given thee in place of water, air, and love, and peace of heart in exchange for bread and beer." To most practical Egyptians, very probably to Ani himself, such sublimated bliss must have seemed a poor substitute for earthly joys. Statues of many of Ani's contemporaries crave no such beatitude, but bear an appeal to the living for "water, a cool breeze, fruits, and all manner of good things" for their lives of "millions of years." Materialistic, perhaps, but to whom is it given to understand eternity?

Although the Egyptians, unlike many ghost-haunted peoples, only rarely revealed a fear of the dead, they greatly feared death with its annihilation of self. That self was a multiple thing, almost unimaginable in disassociation from the body. Since the body obviously became a mere shell in death, its life was believed to depend on a mysterious vital force emanating from god and set in flow at creation to vivify all things, animate and inanimate. This force, called the *Ka,* was universal and indestructible, but it had to have an abode. As it dwelt in the images of the gods in their temples, so it dwelt in the mortal frame of men; hence, the frantic desire of Egyptians to preserve the body and the magical rites performed on the mummy before burial to bring back the life-giving force that had deserted it at death. The Ka shared its corporeal habitation with the *Ba*, a rather earth-bound soul, which could go forth from the living body in dreams and visions and from the mummy to revisit the haunts of life. The Ba was usually pictured as a human-headed bird. Another aspect of the self, the *Akh*, left the body only at death to become a disembodied and transfigured spirit dwelling, not in the mummy or the tomb, but in a blessed state in a vague infinitude such as that pictured to Ani by Atum—an infinitude conceived in much the same way as the watery chaos that had existed before creation.

Since eternity was all but incomprehensible to the Egyptians save in terms of earthly life, continued being seemed impossible without such daily sustenance as that required by living beings. "For thy Ka!" say the guests at funerary feasts, as they raise their cups, "For thy Ka!" as they partake of the viands offered to the dead. Even the gods required food and drink to live, craved as men do amusement and adornment, sweet-smelling ointments and fragrant flowers. Texts of the New Kingdom reveal a struggle between skepticism and belief on the part of many Egyptians, but a desperate hope seems always to have triumphed. All who could afford it furnished their tombs sumptuously with such things as they had enjoyed on earth or hoped to enjoy in the hereafter and left endowments to provide offerings of the necessities of life *in aeternum* and to pay the priests who would perform at their tombs the rites potent for the renewal of vitality.

Since the Egyptian was well endowed with common sense, he was aware that malice or accident or consuming time might thwart the embalmer's skill, that tombs were sometimes robbed, that endowments were diverted and offerings neglected as a man faded from memory; so he embellished his tomb with sculptures and reliefs in his own likeness, where the Ka might take up its abode, and pictured on the walls the things necessary for continued sustenance and pleasure, in the expectation that they would magically come alive. Words had their magic. A man's name might serve as a substitute for his self (the repeated formula, "May his name live forever!" is an evocation of the life force as well as an act of remembrance), and a written or spoken wish or prayer might conjure up the food and drink needed for survival. During the New Kingdom, more and more statues of private persons found their way into the temples, not chiefly as memorials to goodness or greatness, but that their owners, through royal favor, might share forever in the offerings given to gods and deified kings.

Only a privileged few could aspire to immortality under the direct protection of a god. The humble might hope that their masters would need them in eternity as in life. Depicted in the tombs of the great, sometimes even mentioned there by name, they might serve their lords forever. Lacking that, their prayers and the offerings which they could bring out of their poverty might help to secure their futures. Few burials, however humble, lacked some provision for eternity. Even the persons unceremoniously interred, without the long and expensive rites of mummification, in shallow pits at the desert's edge were provided with coarse jars and bowls containing food and drink, with trinkets for their adornment and amulets for their enduring protection. So it had been from remotest prehistoric times, and so it is today, when many Egyptians, Christian and Moslem, bring food offerings to the cemeteries on feast days for the solace of their dead.

CHAPTER SEVEN

The Priests and the People

FROM THE TIME the priestly horologist heralded the dawn on the roof of the great temple at Karnak until the image of the god was retired at nightfall into the temporary death of his golden shrine, the worship of Amun never ceased. Hour by hour, his rites followed a prescribed course. And hour by hour, in other temples throughout Egypt, were celebrated the rites of Amun and the divinities over whom he ruled, with priests and acolytes in perpetual adoration of the mysterious powers that determined the fate of the land. No city was too small to have a temple inhabited by the "living image" of a god. Few deities of the vast pantheon were without their shrines and priestly attendants.

There is a tendency among not a few modern writers to look upon Egypt as priest-ridden, especially to regard the hierarchy of Amun as a sinister force, inimical to the state and oppressive to the people. This is far from the truth. While potentially the clergy, if permitted to control the vast wealth of the gods, might grow to be a menace to the state and ultimately the masses might come to resent their servitude to the gods, in the time of Amunhotep III the power was still firmly vested in the throne; and the people as a whole were indifferent concerning whom they served: they were as well off under one master as another. It is a mistake to think that the priests of Amun were without faith or scruple.

They were traditionalists, upholders of established religion, of which the kingship—the state—was an integral part. Most of them were sincerely, if blindly, orthodox, devout believers in revealed truth, with all its connotations of justice and righteousness. There were worldlings and political schemers among them; there were more than a few who regarded their sacred office chiefly as a means of livelihood; but there were many priests of simple piety, some who experienced a mystic union with deity when they were permitted to "behold the god in his sanctuary."

Two things must be re-emphasized in considering the religion and the priesthood of Egypt. The first is that there was no separation of church and state. This does not mean that Egypt was a theocracy. It means simply, in the words of Kees (*Ancient Egypt*, 266) that "the Egyptians . . . did not regard secular and religious activities as being necessarily opposed to each other. On the contrary, they looked on both as being divinely inspired and performed in the service of the gods; they were, in fact, complementary." As the king was the state, he was also the church. He was ex officio the priest in every temple, solely responsible for maintaining the delicate equilibrium between man and the unseen forces that governed the universe.

The second thing to be remembered is that the temple was not a place of public worship and its priests (serving as the king's proxies) were not shepherds of flocks. The temple was simply the castle in which god dwelt; so it was called, and the priests who officiated in it were called god's servants. They preached no sermons, indeed had no congregation. The great majority of Egyptians never penetrated into the outer courts of the temple; only a very few participated in the rites of its sanctuary, and those who did were admonished to disclose nothing of the mysteries there revealed to them. Not until the Ramesside period is there evidence that less privileged Egyptians were admitted into the temple enclosure. Then they were given access to the outskirts of the sacred precinct so that they might bring their prayers and petitions to the gods and deified kings represented by reliefs on pylons and outer walls and by sculptures in the forecourts. At Karnak, a figure of Ramesses II was known as "Hearer of Prayer," and various great gateways there were designated as "The-Adoration-of-the-People."

Although they had no share in the intimate rites of the temple, Thebans considered themselves fortunate to have the king of the gods dwelling in their midst. His living image protected them from its secret shrine. They had caught glimpses of the shrine as it passed in procession, but they knew, no more than we, what was hidden in it. No cult images have come down to us; and with the single exception of the figure of Min, whose image was openly carried in procession, no representations of cult images appear on temple or tomb walls. The few surviving statues of gods carved in stone come, not from a holy of holies, but from the outer courts of temples, and the many small images of bronze and gilded wood and faïence that crowd our museums are objects of personal piety, made for household shrines or to be offered as ex-votos or worn as amulets. The cult image, doubtless not of great size, was probably fashioned of precious material—of gold, the flesh of the gods—and has long since fallen into impious hands. In any event, it was not holy in itself, but only as the god inhabited it. If the divine Ka entered into the "body" of the god, all was well with the Two Lands. If his worship was neglected, the god might forsake his image and disaster would overtake the people, great and small.

The daily rites performed in the temple were hence directed toward inducing the god to animate his body and toward pleasing him once he was present. Those rites, as practiced in the temple of Amun at Karnak, are in part known to us. We can imagine with some awe similar rites performed day after day and hour by hour in hundreds of temples to invoke the gods to dwell among the people.

At dawn, with veneration, the officiating priest slowly enters the inner sanctuary, prostrating himself many times as he draws near the divinity, breaks the seal on the door of the shrine, and beholds the still lifeless image. Then, with appropriate incantations, in a ceremony similar to that employed for revivifying the mummy at the grave, the figure is magically animated. Amid clouds of fragrant incense and always to the accompaniment of prescribed utterances, the deity is bathed and anointed, clothed and adorned with jewels, garlanded with fresh flowers. Again enthroned in his shrine, the god is presented with offerings of food and drink. All day long the ritual takes its course. The god is entertained with music and dancing, flattered with hymns of praise. He is given, in short, much the same homage as that paid to an earthly ruler, whose very human appetites and passions he is believed to share. At dark, when the sun embarks on its nightly journey through the gloom of the underworld, the priest reverently closes and seals the door of the tabernacle and, backing from the place the god has blessed with his presence, sweeps away the trace of his footprints as he departs.

As has repeatedly been said in these pages, it was theoretically only the reigning king who could officiate in the temple of a god. In earlier, simpler days, rulers may actually have performed their priestly functions in person; but as life grew more complex, it became manifestly impossible for a pharaoh to serve in every temple of every divinity, and priests were appointed to act in the king's stead. "I am the Divine Servant," so the priest announces himself to the god during the daily ritual; "It is the King who sends me to behold thee." Though in theory all clerical appointments were made by the king, he actually chose only a handful among the multitude of Egyptian priests. He selected, undoubtedly with great caution, the High Priest of Amun of Karnak, whom he personally ordained in solemn ceremony, and the High Priests of the Memphite Ptah and of the Heliopolitan Re. He probably appointed the High Priests of certain other major temples, and he also conferred a number of minor benefices on men who had found favor in his eyes. The majority of clerics never came to his notice. Some were appointed by the vizier, some by the High Priest of Karnak; many were chosen by the co-option of the priests of the temples in which they were to serve. A priesthood might be inherited, not by right of law, but by custom, for priests, like lay officials, trained their sons (or their sons-in-law or nephews) to follow in their footsteps; and holy office was often handed down through many generations of a single family. Clerical positions could also be purchased, and it was well worth a man's while to invest his patrimony in return for a lifelong share in the offerings brought to a god.

However priestly office was procured, it was always considered the gift of the king, and it was retained only at his pleasure. What, if any, educational or other qualifications were required of an incumbent is unknown, except that a person with a record of impiety or profanation of a temple or theft of temple property was barred from divine service. It is known that some men gradually advanced to exalted clerical position from the ranks of the minor clergy, but there is no record of previous religious instruction for many of the chief priests who officiated in the mysteries. Though some such instruction must have been given, there were no theological seminaries. The "House of Life," which was attached to each major temple, was apparently primarily a scriptorium where sacred books were transcribed and new religious texts compiled from ancient sources. Its scribes were learned in religious and magical lore and often, since religion and life were inseparable, in what would seem to us secular subjects, such as history, medicine, and mathematics; like the monks in medieval monasteries, they sometimes even wrote down tales and love songs to vary the tedium of their days. While the "House of Life" was hardly a school, it doubtless furnished candidates for the priesthood as it did for officialdom in general. Many laymen served their apprenticeships in such a scriptorium or in one of the numerous administrative offices attached to a temple. Thutmose III himself was educated in the temple of Amun at Karnak. It is possible that his father, Thutmose II, still hoping for a son born of his Great Royal Wife, Hatshepsut, may have destined this son of a concubine for the high priesthood. However that may be, the Conqueror's early training stood him in good stead, for he acquired the backing of the god and the priests, his right to the throne being confirmed (or so he later claimed) by an oracle of Amun.

The hierarchy of the temple of Amun can be taken as typical of that of any major temple, though its priests were more numerous than those of any other sanctuary in the land. At the head was a college of four "Prophets," presided over by the First Prophet, the High Priest. (The word "Prophet" has been passed down from the Greek period, and probably derives from a Heliopolitan priestly title "The Greatest of Seers," "seers" being originally used in the sense of "one who sees," without any implication of foretelling the future.) The duties of the First Prophet of Amun were manifold. He was responsible not merely for the maintenance of the cult, but also for the administration of the great temple complex and the vast domain of the god. In the late Eighteenth Dynasty the supervision of all the temples of Egypt and their priesthoods were frequently in his hands. The other Prophets served as his aides in spiritual and administrative functions, assisted in the latter by numerous laymen who acted as stewards of lands and magazines and workshops. Dr. Hayes has suggested (*Journal of Near Eastern Studies*, Vol. X, [1951], 237–38) that there may have been, in Amunhotep's day, "some sort of nominal division of responsibility between the four prophets of the god—the High Priest presiding at Karnak and delegating the immediate supervision of the Luxor temple, the King's mortuary temple and the Malkata temple to the Second, Third, and Fourth Prophets, respectively."

It was only the prophets who received consecration and were permitted to "see all the manifestations of the god." The clergy included, however, many priests in minor orders, the most numerous among them the *wab*-priests, the "pure" or the "purifiers," who, while not allowed to "open the doors of heaven," acted as deacons to the higher clergy, performing such services as censing and anointing the divine image, caring for the cult objects, and escorting or carrying the bark that contained the god in his shrine. Included among the wab-priests, or allied with them, were clerics of specialized function, such as the lector-priests, guardians and readers of the sacred scrolls; the hierogrammatists, pre-eminently learned in ritual procedure; and the horologists, who determined by the heavens the hours of daily rites and the dates of festivals. The funerary temples on the West Bank of Thebes were similarly organized, but in them was included an order of *sem*-priests, specialized in the cult of the dead, who participated in the rites due departed kings and, against payment, presided at burials and the periodic ceremonies that renewed life for the lesser dead of the necropolis.

Only the higher clergy gave all their time to the god. The minor orders were divided into four shifts, or phyles. Since a phyle served for only a month at a time, the sacerdotal duties of the majority of priests were confined to three months of the year. These months were in the nature of a retreat. During them the priests were held to a most rigorous standard of physical purity. Their heads and bodies were shaven; they were required to perform ablutions at given intervals of the day and night; they could wear only the whitest of linen garments, no wool, no leather—their very sandals were of papyrus; circumcision was obligatory for them; and, of course, during their time of service they could have no relationship with women.

Between his trimestrial periods of attendance on the god, a priest lived a life in the world and of it. Though in the time with which we are concerned it was gradually becoming customary for the cleric who was "off duty" to distinguish himself by his wigless, shaven poll and archaic simplicity of dress, his life otherwise followed much the same course as that of a layman. A humble priest might alternate between temple and field or workshop; a more exalted person might combine priestly functions with those of high administrative office. Consider the priest, says the supercilious scribe: "The Prophet stands as a tenant farmer. The priest performs the service and spends his time soaking himself in the river; he does not distinguish between winter and summer, nor whether the sky be windy and cloudy." Priests were respected by their fellow men chiefly because of their superior position and the emoluments that went with it. Usually chosen "from among the notables" of their locality, they frequently served in administrative councils and law courts. Some were sought after for their learning. There were physicians among them and also astrologers, who determined for the laymen the lucky and unlucky days. They and other priests learned in the ancient writings furnished the people with magical spells against enemies seen and unseen, charms to prevent sickness and injury and dreaded barrenness or to ensure fortune and long life. Those who had "beheld the god" were perhaps revered for that reason alone, but for the most part, a priest was simply a man among men.

There were also priestesses in the service of Amun. They, too, were divided into phyles and subject to strict regulation. They did not participate in the mysteries, but served the god chiefly as musicians and singers. A group of them, headed by "God's Wife," the queen or crown princess (or an appointed substitute), were known as the "Concubines of the God," for Amun, like his royal counterpart, had to have his harem. While Blackman's statement (*Journal of Egyptian Archaeology*, Vol. VII, 9) that "almost all the women living in Thebes or its neighborhood during the New Kingdom

seem to have filled the functions of priestess-musicians" probably is an exaggeration, there is no doubt that the female
attendants of the god were many. Among them were great
ladies and the wives and daughters of priests of all ranks, as
well as some women of apparently humble origin.

In addition to priests and priestess-musicians, no small
number of lay persons were employed in the temple as offering bearers, doorkeepers, butchers and bakers, artists and
craftsmen, and the usual complement of scribes. If one takes
into account the people living on the estates of the god, those
engaged in the collection of his revenues and the care and
distribution of his stores, those who manned his ships and
took part in his trading ventures, Amun was undoubtedly the
greatest single employer of labor in Egypt, second only to the
king. Thebans especially benefited from his presence in their
city. Many of the men prominent in the government doubled
in priestly or administrative offices for the god. In Amunhotep
III's day, one of his viziers, Ptahmose, was also High Priest at
Karnak. The King appointed the wise Amunhotep, son of
Hapu, to serve as First Prophet in the temple of the local god
of Athribis, which he had erected in that city to do honor to
his favorite. While the great architect may possibly have
managed to combine this office with his manifold duties at
Thebes, it is more likely that he sold the living or let it out
on shares to someone on the spot: that this was a common
practice seems evident from the number of priestly titles
frequently borne by a single person.

A large number of Thebans of all classes shared in the
offerings brought to Amun, for clerics and lay employees of
the god were, of course, paid in kind. Surviving fragments
of temple accounts show how carefully the offerings were

apportioned according to the rank of the recipients. While the High Priest had his own estates and an almost royal residence, and the Second Prophet was only less grand, the humblest of the god's servants had to be content with crumbs from the divine table. Late texts in the temple at Edfu exhort the clergy to "lay hands on nothing in [the god's] dwelling," to "open no vessel inside his domain: it is the Lord alone who drinks there." "One lives," it is written, "on the provisions of the gods but one calls provision that which leaves the altar after the Lord has been satisfied." At all periods the tangible wealth of Amun must have proved a temptation to those who served him, but many surely weighed spiritual rewards against temporal gains. "There is no misfortune nor evil for him who lives on [the god's] bounty; there is no damnation for the one who serves him; for his care reaches to heaven, his protection to the earth." "How happy is he that celebrates thy majesty, O great god, and who never ceases to serve thy temple!"

At times of festival, when the offerings reached staggering proportions, even the populace might benefit from them; and Thebes, beyond all other places in Egypt, was festival-happy, with an average of one holy day in three—holy days, for all festivals were religious in nature, though few, if any, of them were marked by undue solemnity. There were no penitential nor expiatory days among them, only days of thanksgiving and praise and jubilation. Even the festivals of the necropolis were happily shared by the living and the living dead.

Festival calendars inscribed on temple walls, the most complete that of Ramesses III at Medinet Habu, give an idea of the great number of Theban feasts. They and pictured scenes in temples and the tombs of nobles help us to visualize the extravagance and pomp with which the feasts were celebrated and provide glimpses of the tumultuous throngs that enjoyed them. The calendars show that by no means all of the Theban festivals were local ones or in honor of the King of the Gods. Many of those which took place in The City were celebrated throughout the Two Lands; and Thebes, as we have seen, honored many gods besides Amun. Most of the feasts, even those of which the origins had long been forgotten, sprang from the soil. Thebes, in common with the rest of Egypt, celebrated seasons of sowing and harvest, the beginning of the year, of the months and the half-months as marked by the phases of the moon. Divinity was in all the changes of the year, and so was the divine kingship, which preserved the balance between man and god-in-nature.

Of all the feasts closely associated with the seasons, that which welcomed the New Year, "the beginning of eternity and the end of everlasting time," was the most joyous. The Egyptian year, which we have inherited, was divided into twelve months, though it knew only three seasons—the Overflowing (of the Nile), the Emergence (of the fields from the flood), and the Drying. New Year's Day, which coincided more or less with the beginning of the inundation, fell around the middle of July; and if the Nile promised to be abundant, there was double cause for rejoicing. In any case, the season was one of hope and promise, and the feast was a royal one. Courtiers came to it bearing gifts for the king; lesser persons exchanged presents and auspicious amulets; the tables of the gods were piled high with good things; lights gleamed from the tombs of the West Bank, where the dead came forth to share in the festivity.

Strangely enough, the Nile was only vaguely a god to the Egyptians, who usually regarded the river as an emanation of another deity, sometimes of Nun, the watery chaos, from which all creation sprang, oftener of Osiris, even (in the New Kingdom) of Amun; and arrogant Thebes then claimed for itself the mysterious source of the river. There is some evidence, however, that in early times sacrifices—including human sacrifices—were made to the Nile as if to a deity in order to ensure a good flood; and a hymn of the New Kingdom praises the river as a god, a nameless god of "no taxes, no levies, no rites, no shrines, no portions, no service . . . who makest men and cattle to live." Always the inundation was greeted with flowers tossed to the waves and with wild festivity.

Many Theban festivals were royal ones. The kings appropriated to themselves, at least in part, those of Horus and of Min; and everybody celebrated with rejoicing anniversaries of the reigning king, his accession, his coronation, his victories, and, above all, his jubilees. For the last-named occasion, notables flocked to Thebes from all of Egypt, and many gods and their attendant priests came in splendid barges. The jubilee, or sed festival, was held at the end of the first thirty years of a pharaoh's reign (though some kings celebrated it earlier) and repeated at shorter intervals thereafter. It was an occasion for renewal of royal vitality and confirmation of the king's god-given right to the Two Lands. Traditionally the sed festival was held at Memphis, the seat of the first kings of united Egypt, but the Thutmosid rulers celebrated it in Thebes, building for it temples or great festival halls and erecting commemorative obelisks in The City and elsewhere. Amunhotep III built at his residence on the West Bank a splendid hall for his first jubilee, where, in the presence of his courtiers and the gods, he re-enacted the drama of the uniting of the Two Lands and received once more the written deed certifying his inheritance. The masses were barred from this dramatic performance, but they could rejoice with their King and watch from the banks the pageantry of arrival and departure on the Nile; and they perhaps received as royal largesse some small part of the abundant food and drink brought from all of Egypt for the occasion. Many hundreds of labels from shattered jars found at the site of the King's palace testify to the great quantity of beer and wine, oils and rendered fats brought to Amunhotep III for his jubilee—a quantity evidently far beyond the needs of his court; and to it must be added the bread and cakes, fruit, vegetables, and meats that poured into the royal storehouses.

The greatest of all festivals were the two feasts of the god Amun, the Beautiful Feast of the Valley and the Feast of Opet. The great god enjoyed other lesser feasts ("How happy is the temple of Amun," wrote a Theban poet, "she who spendeth her days in festival with the King of the Gods within her. . . . She is like to a drunken woman, who sitteth outside her chamber with loosed hair!"), but these two outshone them all. For the Feast of the Valley, the god issued from his castle to visit the funerary temples of earthly kings. It is written that the dead came forth from their tombs to witness his arrival, rejoicing to hear the cries of the crews who manned his barge.

The Theban dead participated in many festivals. There was that of Ptah-Sokar-Osiris, brought to Thebes from Memphis, when the drama of the risen god was re-enacted, and the dead were given symbolic barks, their prows pointed one day to Abydos, the burial place of Osiris, and the next day in the opposite direction for the voyage back to the tomb. There was the Feast of Thoth, who had held the balance at the judgment seat; then the dead, always triumphant, were presented with the Wreath of Justification. There was almost no festival in which the dead were forgotten. But the Feast of the Valley was the great festival of the necropolis and its inhabitants, dead and living. For Thebans, its days were memorial days, occasions for visiting their ancestors, bringing them food, drink, fresh flowers, and lights to dispel the gloom of the tomb.

All feasts, however, even that of the god Min, which was at once a fertility festival and a festival of the royal house, and the riotous feast of Hathor, which had given the name "Drunkenness" to a month of the year, were eclipsed by the Most Beautiful Feast of Opet, when Amun of Karnak visited his Southern Sanctuary at Luxor. It was the longest of all the festivals, lasting ten days in the time of Thutmose III and increasing to twenty-four under the rule of Ramesses III, and it was par excellence the feast of the masses. What significance it had in addition to the divine visit to the harem is unclear. It certainly was associated with the ruling king and may possibly have been a sort of wedding anniversary, a celebration of the mystic marriage of which he was the product, with the queen herself, as "God's Wife," taking part in the rites of the temple. Whatever its import, few kings of the Eighteenth and later dynasties neglected to attend it in person. Though they officiated at some festivals, as at the daily rites of the gods, only by proxy, they never failed to show themselves at Thebes and to its inhabitants for this greatest of all feasts.

Like many other festivals, that of Opet took place during the season of Overflowing, when the rising Nile neared its height. Peasants from the surrounding villages, with work in the fields at a standstill, swarmed into The City; and people, great and small, came from afar to behold the splendor of god and king. That the splendor was indeed surpassing is evident from pictured scenes on temple walls, chief among them that made in the temple of Luxor in the time of Tutankhamun, not improbably after plans drawn up under Amunhotep III. With the help of such scenes and other documents, we can picture the mile-long procession on the Nile, beginning at the Temple of Karnak. The god, in a golden shrine mounted on a portable bark, is carried by white-robed priests to his waiting barge. Other priests purify his path with incense and libation; still others shade him with giant flabella of waving ostrich plumes. His barge, larger than any of the ships that ordinarily ply the Nile, is a temple in miniature, made of the finest woods of Lebanon, sheathed in gold and glittering with jewels. Its prow and stern are adorned with ram's heads wearing the royal crown. On the deck of the barge is a canopied dais on which reposes the shrine. Before the dais, as at the entrance to a temple, are four tall flagstaves fluttering gay pennants and a pair of obelisques sheathed with gold. The shrine is surrounded by statues and royal sphinxes. Among the statues is one of the King holding a golden oar, for it is His Majesty himself who symbolically rows the barge to Luxor. Actually, the cumbersome craft is towed by the royal flagship, manned by high-ranking officials, who have vied with each other for the honor, and it moves upstream only with the aid of crews towing it from the riverbank.

Following the ship of the god come the barges of his consort, Mut, and Khons, his son, somewhat smaller but scarcely less splendidly equipped, and behind and surrounding them is a whole flotilla. Dozens of craft, some with goose heads and tails at bow and stern, escort the procession with music and chanted song. The scene on the riverbank is one of wild confusion, with priests and soldiers, solid citizens and peasants and the Theban rabble, all jostling with one another for a view of the procession. Wild Nubian tribesmen brandish their spears in savage dances, young men and girls leap and twist in acrobatic rhythm; drums boom, trumpets blare, sistra rattle, and chanted hymns rise shrill above the din. In booths set up along the way, petty tradesmen dispense their wares, food and drink and charms and amulets.

All of this seems evident from ancient pictured scenes. One can only imagine the fortune and story tellers, the beggars and charlatans, the sneak thieves and prostitutes, who ply their trades among the crowd; the gaiety rising to hysterical pitch, the shrill quarrels and sordid brawls—all the ingredients of a modern popular festival, in which piety, chicanery and violence, religious ecstasy and eroticism are so often mingled.

At Luxor, fat oxen with gilded horns have been brought for the god's table. Offering bearers come in continuous procession, carrying on their heads trays heaped with good things and wine jars wreathed with flowers. From the temple kitchens issue savory smells of roasting meats and fresh-baked bread and cakes. Now the gods arrive; the King himself leads the divine cortege into the temple. The rites there are guarded from vulgar view, but during the feast days there is no lack of coming and going to amuse the crowd. Perhaps, too, there is a distribution of offerings at the temple gates, after the god has been satisfied.

The prescribed offerings for the Feast of Opet as recorded in the calendar of Ramesses III reached staggering amounts. Daily offerings in the temples and those for minor feasts were modest enough, frequently no more than required for payment of temple personnel. They usually included a few luxury items, such as wine and fruit and fowl, fats and oils to be used in cooking and for lighting; but they were largely confined to the staples, bread and beer, in quantities varying according to the importance of the temple and the feast. The delicacies ultimately went to the dignitaries among the god's servants; the rank and file had to content themselves with bread and beer. For the Feast of Opet, the minimum daily requirement was 11,341 loaves of bread, and 385 jugs of beer, the bread of unusual size and the beer extra strong, whereas the anniversary of the King's coronation was celebrated with only 4,934 loaves and 148 jugs of beer. In addition to these staples, the great feast required beef and game, fat geese and honey cakes, fruits and vegetables, oil and wine, incense and flowers in great quantities. A multitude of workers was required to raise the crops and tend the herds, to bring the offerings to the temple and prepare them for the god's table, to oversee production and distribution, to record—and this was meticulously done—the receipt and distribution of foodstuffs and the many other things necessary to maintain the god in his magnificence and his servants in fitting state.

The average Egyptian, inured to poverty, was content to enjoy vicariously the splendor resulting from his toil. If rarely sated, he was at least not often hungry in the opulent time of

Amunhotep III, and could partake without envy in festivals held in the honor of gods and King. Envy is born of hope or despair; few could hope to rise above their station, but few were desperate. That the wealth of the land was unequally distributed hardly occurred to any Egyptian. If it had been equitably divided, life might have been easier for the majority —but drab. No great temples, the gods forgotten or fled, no glittering festivals to break the monotony of laborious hours and lend a little drunken ecstasy to the humdrum of men's days. No one can be so foolish as to see in ancient Egypt the ideal state, but the old civilization is frequently pictured with too dark a palette. Thebans in the time of Amunhotep III were probably as happy as people of any other time or place. Or is it an error to regard happiness as the ultimate good?

CHAPTER EIGHT

All the King's Men

THOUGH EGYPT WAS AT PEACE during the reign of Amunhotep III, the army built up under former kings had to be maintained; and it was, as has been indicated above, a force to be reckoned with. Until the Eighteenth Dynasty, Egypt had hardly known a professional military class. Previously, kings had their bodyguards, and a small standing army was maintained to man the northern fortresses, erected to protect the borders from marauding tribes, and the strongholds in the south built to guard the trade routes from inner Africa. In addition, there was employed a permanent police force composed of Nubian tribesmen, used chiefly to patrol the desert borders and the cemeteries but also to put down any local disturbances that might occur. In emergency, the pharaohs could call out the militia—men trained in warfare under the nomarchs who, like medieval barons, had their own armed retainers subject to call by the liege lord, the king. The armies thus formed were always small. The olden days in Egypt were, on the whole, peaceful days, marred by little more than raids and counterraids, and until the New Kingdom the pharaohs had conceived no grandiose schemes of foreign conquest.

There was large-scale conscription, it is true, though not chiefly for war. All irrigation work was done by forced labor throughout pharaonic times and for centuries to come (in-

deed until the period of the British occupation), and men
were drafted in great numbers for the quarrying expeditions
and building projects of the kings. These men worked under
military discipline, commanded by an "Overseer of Troops,"
whose title was roughly equivalent to that of general. In the
Eleventh Dynasty a single quarrying expedition into the
Wadi Hammamat is said to have numbered as many as ten
thousand men. Though that figure is surely the result of the
Egyptian passion for large round numbers, the forces employed were doubtless great; and any expedition to a distant
quarry was necessarily accompanied by an armed contingent
to protect the labor gang against raiding nomads. Conscription for mining or quarry duty was dreaded. At best, it meant
hardship, short rations, and thirst; at worst, death far from
home. Today, at Egyptian railway stations, peasant women
who come to see off their menfolk drafted for military service
wail as for the dead. Their wild ululation is an echo from
down a long past, through generations of women mourning
as lost their sons and husbands conscripted for work or war.

By the beginning of the New Kingdom, Egypt had learned
through the Hyksos invasion that she was no longer secure
from attack and that, moreover, her methods of defense were
antiquated. The pharaohs, pursuing the enemy into Asia,
realized that their best safety lay in subjugating the coastal
lands of the Eastern Mediterranean, which offered a spring-
board for aggression. Taking heed of the lessons taught by
more warlike peoples, they built up an ever larger standing
army, well trained, well equipped, and officered by profes-
sionals, who reared their sons to succeed them in military
service.

By the time of Amunhotep III, the home army consisted of

two main corps, each with its own commander, based respectively at Thebes and Memphis. These corps trained troops for foreign service, provided garrisons for frontier fortresses, furnished royal guards and military escorts, and contributed troops for employment on public works. They could also be called upon, if need arose, to supply soldiers for quelling riots or other disturbances of the internal peace; but such matters were, for the most part, handled by the ancient police force, the Medjay, which was now composed chiefly of native Egyptians and officered by Egyptians of military rank.

The army proper was divided into divisions and companies. These were not designated, as is today generally customary, by colorless numbers. The divisions bore the names of the chief gods—"Amun," "Ptah," etc., and the companies were distinguished by pious or picturesque phrases. One company serving under Amunhotep III was called "Manifest-in-Maat," another, "Splendor-of-Aten," and a body of shock troops that campaigned with Thutmose III was known as "Braves-of-the-King." A division numbered about five thousand men and included twenty-five companies of two hundred each, which were further divided into squads headed by petty officers entitled "Commanders of Ten." Both divisions and companies were distinguished by standards, which they bore into battle; to lose these "colors" to the enemy was the greatest of shames.

A small body of chariotry attached to each division served much the same purpose as the armored vehicles of modern times, leading the attack as a cover for the advancing infantry and again appearing at the critical moment of a battle to scatter and pursue the foe. While horse-drawn chariots appear at the very beginning of the Eighteenth Dynasty, the chariotry became an effective arm of the service only with Thutmose III. From that time on, its members formed the elite of the army. They were chosen from among young men of substance, who provided their own equipment and were all honored with the title of "Royal Scribe." Each chariot was manned by a driver and a fighter, and the squadron was led in battle by the royal equipage. The title of "Charioteer of the King" was one of the proudest. The bearer of it not only accompanied the pharaoh in the field, but frequently was sent into distant lands on royal misisons, acting as a sort of ambassador-at-large. On retirement, he might look forward to an especially high position in the king's household.

As has ever been the case, it was the infantry that was the backbone of the army. The foot soldiers were headed by a company of shock troops composed of seasoned veterans, who bore the brunt of the attack. There were companies of archers, armed with strong bows and wearing axes and daggers at their belts. There were spearmen, bearing shields of oxhide and spears sometimes nearly six feet long; there were soldiers armed only with axes and clubs. Though kings and princes are frequently pictured in scale armor and remains of such armor, with metal scales sewn to a linen or leather doublet, have been found, the common soldier had little protection, save, rarely, a leather apron. He fought with uncovered head, and his dress hardly differed from that of the ordinary peasant—a short kilt or occasionally a tunic. Sometimes a soldier could be distinguished by his haircut or the cut of his kilt or by a bandolier; frequently, he could not be told from a worker in the fields.

The army was composed in part of professional soldiers and in part of conscripts. There was a draft quota. "I mustered the young men of my Lord," wrote Amunhotep, son of Hapu, as Scribe of Recruits. "My pen reckoned the number of millions. I inducted the sturdiest men from the seat of their families. . . . I levied the estates according to their numbers. . . . I filled out the ranks with the best of the captives that His Majesty had taken on the battlefield."

Until the time of Amunhotep III, the army had been made up chiefly of native Egyptians, always with a good sprinkling of Nubians and only occasionally a few Asiatics, but now, numbers of Eastern prisoners of war or their descendants were impressed into service; now also for the first time, there appear among the forces the mysterious "Sherden," a roving sea people thought by some to have been the ancestors of the Sardinians. Apparently none of these aliens was a mercenary in the true sense of the word; they were captives who had bought their freedom by a change of allegiance. It was not until later that Egyptian kings had to resort to hiring foreigners to fight their battles and protect their thrones.

The pharaoh was, of course, commander-in-chief of the army, his vizier, the minister of war. While the warrior kings of the Eighteenth Dynasty told of campaigning at the head of their troops and not rarely boasted of their exploits single-handed against the enemy, one wonders how many of them actually led their men into action. There is no evidence of an Egyptian ruler's ever having been killed or wounded or taken prisoner. But then, Egyptian accounts never mention defeat, much less losses of men or equipment; and pictured scenes show only the slain enemy, never a fallen Egyptian warrior. His Majesty is always held to be victorious. Though rare sources indicate that such was not always the case, the kings of the Thutmosid line seem, on the whole, to have been valiant and successful in warfare. In consultation with their chiefs of staff they planned their campaigns well. A battle was no longer the primitive free-for-all that it had been in the past. Troops were deployed to tactical advantage and a carefully planned strategy was devised to outwit the enemy. It seems a bit bold to assume that warfare was always or usually the chivalrous affair described (or rather, perhaps, recommended) by the Nubian Piankhi, who conquered Egypt in the eighth century B.C. On a famous stela which he erected in the Temple of Amun at Napata, he records his victorious campaign in Egypt and sets down his rules for combat. Under Piankhi, apparently, there was no attack by night nor surprise by day. Rival commanders agreed on the place and hour of battle, launching their troops into the fray only at a pre-arranged signal. Piankhi charged his officers to allow the enemy time to bring up reinforcements, if those were needed, trusting always that Amun would be on the right side. Thutmose III, however, seems certainly to have recognized the value of surprise attack; and as reliefs showing heaped-up heads and hands bear witness, warfare in general was neither chivalrous nor pretty; there was frequently little quarter given.

The rewards for military service were great. Like everyone else in Egypt, officers and men were paid in kind, according to their rank; but valiant officers were frequently compensated with lands and captive slaves and costly decorations and could look forward on retirement to positions of honor, frequently to posts in the household of the king. Promotions were often made from the ranks for bravery in the field, and even common soldiers of the regular army were accorded preferential treatment at home in the way of housing and allotments in return for rearing sons for the service. Conscripts probably got no more than they were accustomed to having in civil life—a bare living; and after service, most of them returned to their usual drudgery. In the field, however, anyone could anticipate a share in the booty captured from the enemy. Slaves, horses, cattle, fine clothes and rich accouterments, jewelry, food and wine in abundance—any of these might fall to a soldier's lot.

Since campaigns in Syria were limited to the summer months, when the Egyptian crops had been harvested and the Nile was in flood but the fruits and grain of the enemy were still ungarnered, the provisioning of the invading army was not too serious a problem. Though the troops in Syria may sometimes have gone on short rations, pillage was the accepted rule, and the hungry peasant-conscript might on occasion experience an abundance of food such as he had never previously known. While all spoils, like all victories, were the pharaoh's and granted to others only through his bounty, even the great conqueror Thutmose III could not preserve discipline in the face of the temptation offered to his forces by Syrian loot. He failed in his first attempt at capturing the stronghold of Megiddo because "the army of His Majesty had . . . given up their hearts to plundering the things of the enemy," and he was obliged to put off for a season his investment of Kadesh because the troops found Phoenician gardens filled with fruit and vats overflowing with new wine: "Behold, the army of His Majesty was drunk and anointed with oil every day as at a feast in Egypt."

With such dazzling rewards in view, there should have been no lack of volunteers for the army; but the Egyptians were never by nature a warlike people, and besides, there was a darker side to the picture. Though most of our information about a soldier's life is furnished by the inevitable scribe writing in praise of his own calling, the picture he paints is probably hardly more grim than the reality. Army discipline was enforced by the lash. The recruit, scarcely more than a child, was shut up in barracks, where he was beaten until he was stiff, "like papyrus that is pounded into sheets." When he went off to service in Syria, he marched "laden like an ass" with his arms and ration of bread and a skinful of "stinking" water. The road was difficult. From the last Egyptian outpost, it was a ten- to twelve-day march across a waterless waste before reaching the wells of Palestine. The way was beset by Bedouin tribes, who took advantage of every lapse in vigilance, and the footsoldiers halted only to mount guard. The bones of not a few of them were left to whiten in the wilderness.

In the course of the wars of Thutmose III, Egypt became a sea power, dominating the Eastern Mediterranean with her fleet. There are no records of naval battles until the Ramesside period, but the great conqueror and his successors employed ships as transports for carrying at least part of their forces and supplies to Syrian harbors. The recruit fared somewhat better at sea than on land. While he was crowded with his company into a vessel about two hundred feet long and only about sixty feet wide, the voyage was a short one. Aided by favorable winds and currents, it usually required only a couple of days, though the return trip meant eight or nine days of what must have been misery. Once in Syria and in the presence of the enemy, the poor soldier was "a trapped bird," his legs "turned to water." If he escaped death and again saw home, he as likely as not returned slung across a donkey, sick and miserable, to be bedridden and no better than a "stick of worm-eaten wood." Even a charioteer, who had invested his patrimony in a splendid equipage, could fare badly. Sometimes he became tangled in his reins and was thrown among thorns and bitten by stinging scorpions; and when he limped back to his base, bruised and torn, he was rewarded for the loss of his equipment with a beating.

The army scribes themselves suffered. Those who remained at home at headquarters or in the war office had an easy time of it, but those who accompanied the army in the field might share the hardships of the troops. Scribes prided themselves on their knowledge of Syrian geography and the difficult terrain fought over by the forces of the pharaohs, and ostentatiously larded their writings with foreign words and phrases; but a quartermaster's clerk could meet with disgrace for failure to estimate properly the supplies needed for a body of troops or to have the customary bread and beer delivered at the appointed place and time. A scribe might be obliged, moreover, to brave the perils of the wild Syrian mountains, covered with forbidding forests that darkened the noonday sky. He had to traverse in his chariot perilous, boulder-strewn trails bordering deep ravines, in terror of wild beasts and roving tribesmen. He traveled bow in hand, threatened by day with death at the hands of an ambushed foe "seven to nine feet tall," and plundered of his equipment by night as he slept. If he found a girl to console him at the end of his journey, he got into trouble for that.

While the scribes report in detail the hardships of army life, they have little to say about a sailor's lot. Ships and sailors were perhaps a commonplace to them. From the beginning of time, boats had been the chief means of transportation on the country's one great highway, the Nile; and Egyptians had acquired great skill in building and navigating both river craft and seagoing vessels. Troops were carried by water for the subjugation of Nubia, and the early kings of the Eighteenth Dynasty used Nile boats for the conquest of the Hyksos and their native collaborators. The great problem in almost treeless Egypt was to get wood for shipbuilding. An important part of the Nubian tribute was timber, and from early times, as we have seen, one of the chief articles of trade with Asia was wood, no small part of which was used in the construction of vessels.

Several types of ships, exclusive of the skiffs and small craft that crowded the Nile, were in current use. Large boats for river travel were light and of shallow draft for navigation among shoals and rapids. Their cabins were built high to command a view of the shores for a long distance. They were equipped with sails, but these were effective only in favorable winds; in calm or against the wind and among rapids, the crews had to go ashore and resort to the use of tow ropes. Ships engaged in traffic with the incense ports of the Red Sea were built for speed, with long lines and huge sails, for the seaway skirted almost harborless desert coasts that offered neither food nor water. Vessels constructed for the Mediterranean were larger and broader of beam. Both types of seagoing vessel had but one great sail and a single row of oarsmen. While the ships used as transports were commanded by experienced navigators, there was little differentiation between army and navy personnel: both officers and men were amphibious. The highest titles of the navy, "Overseer of Ships" or "Overseer of all the Ships of the King," were borne by men who, like the "ruler of the Queen's Navee," apparently had no naval experience whatever, but served in a purely administrative capacity. Like the regiments and companies of the army, the ships of the line had resounding names, "The Ruler-is-Strong," "Beloved-of-Amun," "Star-in-Memphis." The flagship of Amunhotep III was called, like his palace, "Splendor-of-the-Aten."

There is no way of telling how large the combined forces of the pharaohs were at any time during history. It has been assumed, on what seems to be rather flimsy evidence, that in the New Kingdom one man in ten was conscripted. The statement on which this assumption is based is in the Papyrus Harris, where Ramesses III declares that he, unlike former kings, did not exact a tithe from the personnel of any temple for appointment to the infantry or chariotry. (Breasted, *Ancient Records*, IV, 178). The temples may well have enjoyed a privileged position under those "former kings," and the proportion of men conscripted for the army from the population as a whole may well have been greater than one in ten, especially in times of war. These figures, moreover, even if reliable, would get us nowhere, since the total population of Egypt at any period of the past is—and is likely to remain —in the realm of the unknown.

When one stands dwarfed before the colossi of Amunhotep III or as a midget in the colonnade of his Luxor temple, the past looms disproportionately large. Egypt, one thinks, must have been inhabited by swarming millions to have produced such mighty works without the aid of modern equipment or machinery, and Thebes must have been almost as populous as one of today's great capitals. The vainglorious inscriptions relating the conquests of the ancient pharaohs, listing thousands of captives and tons of booty, lead one to imagine vast armies besieging Syrian cities hardly less great than Thebes itself. It is hard to imagine that Palestine and Syria together covered an area less than that of present-day Kansas, much of it uninhabitable, and that the cultivable land of Egypt in the Eighteenth Dynasty could easily have been contained within the boundaries of Connecticut. As for Thebes, it would be rated today as little more than a prosperous provincial town.

There is no doubt that in antiquity the population of Egypt fluctuated widely from period to period, as it has down to recent times, in accordance with the stability of the government and the vagaries of the Nile. Modern scholars think that in the Old Kingdom the country may have numbered two million inhabitants; Winlock estimated that at the beginning of the Eleventh Dynasty, after the disturbances of the First Intermediate Period, the population had dropped to little more than a million. Breasted believed that during the prosperity of the New Kingdom, the numbers increased to five or six million. Classical writers, basing their beliefs on tales of past glory told to them in the age of Egypt's decline, raised the figure to seven or eight million, a figure that Diodorus Siculus (I, 21) found had diminished to three million in his day, shortly before the time of Christ. Under the Romans, the acreage was increased, and with it perhaps also the population. There were elaborate censuses of population in pharaonic times, but no cumulative figures have come down to us. There were also censuses under the Ptolemies and the Romans, but again no complete record of them remains.

It must be remembered that Egypt was always an agricultural country entirely dependent on the annual flood of its mighty stream and that ancient irrigation at its best was able to reach far less territory than is cultivated today. The country was, and is, in the well-worn phrase, the "gift of the river," but it was a gift given only in exchange for unceasing labor and wise provision against periods of dearth. Pharaoh's dream, as recorded in the biblical story of Joseph, might well have been the recurrent nightmare of any thoughtful ruler; for long failure of the Nile could bring in its wake not only famine and disease and death, but perhaps even rebellion on the part of men driven to desperation by hunger. More rarely, an over-high Nile, sweeping away dikes and fields and cattle, entire villages and their inhabitants, could prove equally disastrous. Ancient records usually give only the bright side of life in the Nile Valley. Although the reiterated statement of kings and governors that "no one was hungry in my time" provides negative evidence of periods of scarcity, and a few texts refer more or less openly to famine, such evidence of divine displeasure and royal inadequacy as dearth and disease is usually only hinted at or passed over in silence.

Dearth and disease there has always been in Egypt. Classical writers record disastrous famines due to failure of the inundation; so do Arab historians such as Abd el-Latif, who reported a famine of the twelfth century during which, in the ancient literary phrase, starving men "ate their own children." Breakdown of the central government, with consequent relaxation of irrigation work and depletion of public stores of grain, also meant hunger. It is possible, moreover, that Egypt may have suffered from seismic disturbances such as are believed to have devastated anciently the Near East (always, as today, in the earthquake belt), leaving disaster in their wake. Egyptian texts have nothing to say concerning such acts of God. They are also reticent about disease, which was probably as effective in keeping down the population as it has been within memory. There is evidence that bilharziasis, the parasitic disease that still weakens and ultimately kills so many of the peasantry, existed in pharaonic times, as did also the scourge of smallpox; medical papyri indicate the prevalence of pulmonary ailments; in certain ancient cemeteries hasty burials hint at epidemics, so also do vague references to pestilence. Indeed, the myth of the ravening Hathor bent on the destruction of mankind may be a folk memory of some devastating "Black Death" of antiquity. There is no reason, moreover, to believe that infant and child mortality was much less in the past than at present, when Egypt has one of the highest rates in the world. "When death comes," an ancient sage reminds us, "he steals away the infant that is on its mother's lap, like him who has reached old age."

While any estimate is hazardous, it is doubtful that the population in the Eighteenth Dynasty numbered more than four million persons, if, indeed, it ever reached that figure. A recent guess by Dr. Klaus Baer (*Journal of the American Research Center in Egypt*, Vol. I, 1962) places the cultivable land in the New Kingdom at six million arouras (around four million acres, and thus about two-thirds of the present arable area), the agricultural population at three million, and the total population at four and a half million. The French savants who accompanied the Napoleonic expedition to Egypt early in the nineteenth century estimated the total arable land at about four and a half million acres, with only about three and a half million actually under cultivation, and the total population at only two and a half million. Edward William Lane, writing in 1835 (*The Manners and Customs of the Modern Egyptians*, [London, 1836]), gives the same figure as the official estimate of population for that year but doubts that the inhabitants actually numbered as many as two million, although in his opinion, the land was capable, if wisely administered, of supporting double that number. When he wrote, conditions were much the same as they had been in antiquity.

The great Aswan dam and the Nile barrages had not been built to store water for perennial irrigation and thus to increase the acreage yielding more than a single annual crop. Methods of agriculture were little different from those of pharaonic times. The Delta, that most fertile region of Egypt, was still largely unreclaimed—only half of it is cultivable today, and much of the reclamation has been accomplished in the present century. There was more small manufacture than in pharaonic times, but this advantage was offset by the export of raw cotton and especially of grain, the profits from which went into a few well-lined pockets and did nothing to alleviate the condition of peasant and workman, who had profited little enough from the wealth of the Eighteenth Dynasty. Even in Lane's hungry period, Egypt could support a number of sizable towns and two considerable cities—Cairo, with a population of about a quarter of a million, and Alexandria, with something over a hundred thousand inhabitants. It seems possible that greater Thebes during the prosperity under Amunhotep III may have been at least as large as Cairo was in the poverty of the early nineteenth century.

Of the official total of two and a half million inhabitants in 1835, Lane estimated somewhat less than half to be males, about four hundred thousand (one-third) of whom were of an age for military service. Half that many men were actually in the armed forces of Mohammed Ali. It is improbable that any ancient pharaoh in his wildest flights of fancy envisaged an army of two hundred thousand, much less the army of a million men ascribed by Strabo (17.1.46) to the Theban kings. Alexander the Great conquered his world, it is said, with thirty or forty thousand men; Caesar had about the same number for the subjugation of Gaul; the legions that maintained the far-flung Roman Empire under Augustus apparently totalled no more than two hundred thousand soldiers; and to come closer home in time and place, six thousand Normans under William the Conqueror took and held England from the Clyde to the Welsh border. (England in the eleventh century was, like Syria in the New Kingdom, sparsely populated and divided into what might almost be considered petty states of differing racial origin and administrative custom.)

If the ancient records can be relied upon, the forces of Ramesses II engaged at the battle of Kadesh consisted of four divisions, that is, twenty thousand men; with reserves, he might possibly have had thirty thousand soldiers in the field. If we assume a round number of four million inhabitants for Egypt in the Eighteenth Dynasty and accept the rather dubious statement that one man in ten was drafted, that would mean (basing our figures on Lane's calculation of males available for military service in 1835, as given above) a conscript army of about fifty to sixty thousand men, to which an uncertain number of professional soldiers should be added, bringing the total probably as high as seventy thousand, certainly more than enough for field duty, garrisons at home and abroad, royal guards and escorts, and labor on public works. It must again be stated that wars were fought, quarrying expeditions undertaken, and most buildings erected during the season of the inundation, when agricultural work was at a standstill and consequently there were great numbers of idle men;

and it must be remembered that the work in fields and gardens was shared, as it still is, by women and children and the aged and infirm. Probably few ancient rulers were as unwise as the Khedive Ismail, who a century ago impounded peasantry for labor on the Suez Canal at a time when the grain still stood unharvested in the fields; but all of them took advantage of the manpower left idle during the annual flood. Great builders such as Amunhotep III may have borrowed workers from the land at other seasons. There is some evidence that a labor shortage, which became acute under the Ramessides, was beginning to be felt in his time. And this very shortage may be evidence that the population of Egypt never exceeded the figure of four million which we have suggested for the New Kingdom at its height.

Today, Egypt is one of the most densely populated countries in the world, with an estimated twenty-eight million inhabitants. As one travels up the Nile Valley, one never sees from dawn to dusk a landscape empty of human beings. Cairo is a swarming city of over two and a half million persons; Alexandria numbers more than a million. Though the great enemy, famine, has been largely defeated by perennial irrigation and the extension through irrigation and drainage of cultivable lands, the present acreage is not sufficient to support the people. Forty to sixty per cent of the necessary breadstuffs must be imported, and still the majority of Egyptians live at a bare subsistence level. The new high dam, with its promise of two million additional acres of arable land and water power for industry, may improve the condition of the Egyptians. It may, on the other hand, result in a further increase in population and crowding into city slums, rather than a surcease from grinding poverty.

CHAPTER NINE

The Great Heresy and Its Aftermath

IN THE THIRTY-SEVENTH or thirty-eighth year of his reign, Amunhotep III died and was buried with suitable pomp in his unfinished tomb in the Valley of the Kings. Though he was hardly in his mid-fifties, modern historians are unanimous in referring to him as an old man; and there seems little doubt that he was prematurely aged, perhaps even senile, as the result of excess and sickness. He was succeeded by the son of his Great Wife Tiy, who came to the throne as Amunhotep IV but is better known to history as Akhenaten.

The new King was not a prepossessing figure. Sculptured likenesses from a Theban shrine which he erected in the second year of his reign show him with brutal realism as grossly emasculate, with the swelling hips and belly and breasts of a woman, but with sunken chest, skinny neck, and spindly shanks. In the far from pleasant features of his narrow face—coarse nose and lips, almost mongoloid eyes, and long, stubborn chin—sensuality and fanaticism seem to struggle for dominance. These representations and later portrayals in similar style have been cited as examples of Akhenaten's passion for truth. They seem rather to indicate a total lack of self-irony.

Akhenaten has come down in history as the first monotheist. He is today widely known for his vain attempt to clear Egyptian religion of the debris of ages and to substitute one god, the Aten, the visible disk of the sun, for the vast pantheon. He has become a legendary figure, shrouded in half-truths and myth. In scholarly circles an endless and often bitter controversy is waged over the interpretation of the meager records of his reign. Arguments wax hot about whether or not the young King shared the throne of his father as co-regent during the latter's declining years. Historians indulge in widely divergent speculations concerning the tangled relationships of the royal family. They offer the most disparate estimates of the motives and character of the unfortunate ruler who was mentioned in later Egyptian records (when at all) only as "that enemy from Akhetaten."

The main facts concerning the King and his career can be briefly stated. He was crowned Amunhotep IV, but by the sixth year of his reign (or toward the end of his co-regency with his father), he had changed his name from Amunhotep, "Amun Is Pleased," to Akhenaten, "Serviceable-to-the-Aten." In the same year, he journeyed down the Nile and marked out on the site now known as Amarna the city of Akhetaten, "Horizon of the Aten," which he destined for his capital. Since the region was wasteland, he claimed that it had belonged to his god from the beginning of time and set up boundary stelae to mark its limits. On these stelae, he vowed never to exceed the limits thus set: "May he [the King] sojourn here," later prayed one of his followers, "until the swan turns black and the crow white, until the hills arise to depart and the water flows upstream." By his eighth year, the King and his court were settled in the new capital, which has been summarily described in Chapter III, where he erected new stelae reaffirming his oath.

He was already married to Nefertiti, the beautiful. Her

antecedents are unknown. Among the many guesses concerning her origin, one of the most plausible is that she was Akhenaten's cousin, the daughter of Ay, who was possibly a brother of Queen Tiy and certainly a power behind the throne during the reign of Akhenaten and his successors. He himself ruled briefly as the last king of the Eighteenth Dynasty. Nefertiti bore six daughters, one of whom died young and two of whom were married to Akhenaten's immediate successors, Smenkhkare and Tutankhamun, putative sons of Amunhotep III, although if the latter was related to him at all, he was more likely (unless an extraordinarily elastic chronology is employed) to have been his grandson. While the beautiful Nefertiti was accorded more prominence in pictorial and written records than any of her predecessors, including Queen Tiy, she apparently fell from favor in Akhenaten's twelfth year of rule, and was relegated to the palace that had been built for her in the northern suburb of Amarna, which offers some evidence of her sojourn, none of her ultimate fate.

Her place in Akhenaten's affection, together with many of her epithets, seems to have been usurped by her son-in-law Smenkhkare, who disappeared from history in the third year of his reign, during part or all of which he may have acted as co-regent. Akhenaten died after seventeen years on the throne. The manner of his death and his place of burial are unknown, though speculation is rife over remains hastily interred with remnants of royal trappings in Tomb Fifty-five of the Valley of the Kings.

It has been suggested that Akhenaten's hegira from Thebes may have been by agreement with the priests of Amun, who undoubtedly thought him better out of the way. Whatever the facts—and they are definitely not known—it seems obvious that Thebes, with its strongly entrenched adherents to the ancient faith, was no place from which to launch a religious revolution. Few representatives of old Theban families followed the King to his new capital. The majority of his officials were parvenus—soldiers, household officials, scribes, architects, and not a priest among them. They boasted of their obscure origins in the tombs granted to them in the cliffs of Amarna. "I was a man of low birth," says one, "but the King established me, caused me to associate with princes and companions, gave me provisions every day—I, who had been one that begged bread!" Another, a priest of the Disk, prays to Akhenaten as "the god who formed me, fostered me, fed me, provided me with goods . . . . Thou didst bring me to the front from the rear," he adds, "making me powerful when I was of no account." Whether such men were loyal to the King and the Aten through convicition or self-interest must remain forever uncertain. Some of them suffered disgrace before Akhenaten's brief rule was over. A few were apparently faithful to the end. Still fewer survived the King to play a part in the subsequent history of Thebes.

Akhenaten did not succeed in establishing his god without a struggle. While he had erected shrines to the Aten in Thebes during the early years of his rule, the worship of the old gods still continued. But after his removal to the new capital, he sent his cohorts far and wide in an attempt to eradicate all traces of the ancient faith. Although they ranged from Memphis far into Nubia, their venom was vented chiefly on Thebes and Amun. Temples were closed, their cult images destroyed, their wealth diverted to the new capital and the new god. The King's bullies swarmed through the Theban necropolis, entering rich tombs (and perhaps looting them en route) to hack out all reference to the old deities. Private names—even royal names—compounded with that of Amun were systematically obliterated. The City must have experienced great terror, but there is no evidence that Akhenaten's rabble met with any resistance. The faithful adherents of the old religion must simply have gone underground. That there were such among the priestly and official families seems clear from the alacrity with which the ancient worship was reinstated after Akhenaten had disappeared from the scene. As for the populace, they were apparently little moved by the storm that raged above them. In Amarna itself, the necropolis workers still cherished their amulets of the good Bes and Tauret, of the protecting Eye of Horus.

In view of the piety and stubborn conservatism of the Egyptians, it is to be wondered that Akhenaten's revolution could succeed even temporarily. There is evidence that he may have had the support of certain elements of the army, which seized their chance of gaining control of the government; it may well be that his iconoclasts were recruited from the horde of soldiers and foreign conscripts left idle during long years of peace. Probably an ingrained reverence for the divinely ordained kingship aided in holding revolt in check. It may also be, as has been suggested, that a natural portent—famine, pestilence, or earthquake—frightened Egyptians into a suspicion that the old gods had deserted them and into a desperate acquiescence to the will of the King. Any or all of these factors may have been involved. All that can be said with certainty is that Akhenaten managed to remain on the throne for seventeen years.

They seem to have been years of administrative disintegration and economic distress. One can well imagine that the collapse of the traditional religion left impoverished great numbers of persons who had been dependent on the temples. While the peasants continued to work the fields of the former gods for the profit of the King and the Aten, and large numbers of artists, craftsmen, and laborers found employment at Amarna and in the construction of shrines to the Disk erected by Akhenaten elsewhere in Egypt, the vast personnel formerly employed directly or indirectly in temple service could hardly have been absorbed.

We know of the state of Egypt during the religious revolution only from sparse and hardly disinterested records of the counterrevolution, but contemporary archaeological evidence seems to indicate that all may not have been well with the land. The remains of Akhetaten give the impression that it was an embattled city, a luxurious concentration camp. Along the encircling cliffs that formed its natural fortifications can still be seen the track worn by the weary feet of sentries who guarded the King and his followers. Below, at the edge of the desert plain, a long line of barracks for foot soldiers and chariotry protected the city still further, and one can well believe that boats patrolled the river to defend any approach to the capital from the west. While Akhenaten's vow never to pass the limits set by his boundary stelae may have been simply a legal phrase used to define property rights, there is no hint that he ever left his capital once he had taken up residence there.

He seems to have lived in complete isolation from reality. The encroachments of the Hittites into northern Syria and the frantic pleas of Egypt's Asiatic allies apparently left him unmoved. The eastern empire gradually slipped away; by the time of his death, the hard-won control of the pharaonic armies did not extend beyond southern Palestine. Some scholars have regarded Akhenaten's attitude toward Asia as evidence of a convinced pacifism. It was probably the result of inertia—and of troubles nearer at hand. It was no mean task he had set himself, that of eradicating in a lifetime a tradition reaching back into a past beyond memory.

At this distance, the real character of Akhenaten defies analysis. One school of contemporary thought sees in him the inspired prophet of the One God, a god of all-embracing love and universal peace. In certain liberal churches his story is told with reverence, almost as if he were a forerunner of Christ. Another school, at present very fashionable, regards him with some disgust as a degenerate, at best as an ineffectual weakling. The truth probably lies between the two extremes.

The representations of the King certainly suggest a physical degeneracy of the sort that is frequently accompanied by a brilliant, if unstable, mind. There is small doubt that Akhenaten had vision. The monotheistic religion he sought to impose on Egypt had, in contrast with the involuted traditional faith, the grandeur of simplicity. He had vision and, as Sir Alan Gardiner has said, he had courage. But his vision was limited and his courage was the blind daring of fanaticism. The Aten, with its rays ending in blessing hands, was quasi-anthropomorphic (for it is given to few to conceive deity save in their own likeness), but it was, nevertheless, remote and impersonal, more distant from mankind than the very human old gods had been. There was still no question of popular participation in the cult. The King was sole mediator between God and man. He was the son of the Aten, as his ancestors had been sons of Amun-Re. Even more: while his father had set himself up as a god, Akhenaten went a step farther—he was the One God. He and his family alone were pictured as receiving the gift of life from the Aten, and his followers prayed to him and the Disk in the same breath. The King offered the god the symbolic figure of Maat. That figure was the same old Maat, not factual truth, but divine order; only the order was now of the King's own devising, not that handed down through the long line of royal ancestors. One of Akhenaten's great errors in judgment lay, as Peet long ago remarked, in thinking he could balance two decades of monotheism against two thousand years of tradition.

Some such balance might possibly have been attained had the new religion proffered anything that was really new, but it destroyed without building. As it offered the people no participation in its mysteries, so it offered no spiritual guidance, no rule of conduct. Above all, it offered small comfort. While tombs were built during the Amarna period, bodies mummified and laid to rest with appropriate and, to some extent, traditional ceremonies, Osiris, both as judge and savior, recedes into shadow along with the other gods. Though he seems not to have met with the vindictive official hatred accorded to Amun, for the most part he suffered the obloquy of silence. It is true that the dead were sometimes promised eternal existence by favor of the King, sleeping the sleep of death by night in their tombs but awakened each morning to breathe in the life offered them by the vivifying rays of the Aten. Those favored men who were granted burial in the rock-tombs of Amarna might go forth by day to serve the Disk in his temple, to haunt, unseen, the fair villas and gardens they had made in Akhetaten, until sunset recalled them to their eternal homes. But there was now only one road to bliss; it was closed to all save the followers of the Aten, and the only righteousness and its chief reward seemed to lie in perpetual adoration of the God-King.

As has been indicated in the course of this study, there was always in the background of Egyptian religious thought a hazy, monotheistic idea, in which the sun usually emerged as the creator of all things. Before Akhenaten's time, the Disk had entered the pantheon and had been hospitably received as a visible aspect of the life-giving sun. It has been suggested that Akhenaten was inspired from the East, where many peoples adored the sun, and that he therefore chose as his sole god a deity that would be acceptable, not only to vassal countries of Asia but also to the native Egyptians of his time, infiltrated by and intermarried with foreigners. Although traditional religion may well have been to some extent undermined by contact with a world that flourished under gods other than Egypt's, it seems hardly necessary to look so far afield for the source of the King's inspiration. His vision of a sole god appears to have been a natural outgrowth of the very ancient Heliopolitan sun religion. From earliest times, that religion had penetrated other Egyptian theologies, and during the Eighteenth Dynasty it had gained in strength. The temple which Akhenaten raised to the Disk at Amarna was very like the sun-flooded temples built by Fifth Dynasty kings in honor of Re.

The beautiful and often quoted hymn, which the young Pharaoh himself is thought to have written in praise of the Aten, has forerunners in praise of Amun-Re which are only less lovely. That hymn has been cited to show that Akhenaten's god was a god of universal brotherhood. It actually says little more than that the sun gives life to men and beasts everywhere. There is no evidence that Akhenaten was any more concerned with the clamoring Asiatics who begged his bounty and assistance against the Hittites than he was with his people as a whole—and that, apparently, was not at all.

The new religion brought with it no administrative reforms, no alleviation of the condition of the masses. On the contrary, if one can judge from scant documents of the following periods, it resulted in the breakdown of the machinery of government and general hard times. The King was as aloof from common life as any of his predecessors had been. While sculptures and reliefs portrayed his physical idiosyncracies and the domesticity of the royal family with frankness and shockingly bad taste, no one dared to presume on the intimacy thus invited. Courtiers bowed lower than ever before, and commoners still kissed the dust before a sovereign who seemed to have small doubt that he and his god were one. The extravagance of the court was no less than it had been in the past, and its luxury was still maintained at the expense of the populace.

It became increasingly a court of dark intrigue, permeated by a miasma of decay. The general malaise is evident in the art of Amarna. Like the new religion, the art sought freedom from the binding conventional forms of the past. It is full of sunshine and flowers, of genre scenes executed with liveliness and frequently with humor; but for all its febrile charm, much of it breathes decadence in every line. One suspects some artists of working tongue in cheek. From the rubbish of Amarna come little sculptured groups of affectionate monkey families, unmistakable caricatures of the royal ménage.

In its often almost expressionistic freedom, the art of Amarna has an especial appeal to us who are living in the present; but while traces of its influence linger into the early Nineteenth Dynasty, the reaction back to traditional forms was not long in making itself felt. For the most part, the result was not a happy one. In pre-Amarna periods, the best of the works that followed the age-old canons were imbued with life—character or action caught at a swiftly arrested moment; but in the times following the great schism, the formula became more and more stereotyped. Some sculptured work of the early Ramesside period, especially royal work, was very beautiful, and certain architectural monuments showed both grandeur and inventiveness. But little by little, art coarsened into the mechanical and banal. The lively scenes of daily life in private tombs were gradually replaced by magical pictures and texts from religious works to aid the deceased in his perilous quest for immortality. The spontaneity and invention that had once operated within the traditional framework all but disappeared. The ancient vitality occasionally reasserted itself, but art as a whole became the expression of a tired and listless civilization.

The disappearance of Akhenaten from the scene did not mean, as has sometimes been stated, the immediate release of the vengeance of the followers of Amun and the summary destruction of the city of the Aten. Akhenaten's successor, Smenkhkare, if he ruled at all in his own right, may have made his peace with Thebes, but apparently the next king, Tutankhamun (born Tutankhaten), abandoned the new capital only in the fifth year of his brief reign. Even then, houses and palaces were left standing: villas were carefully locked as if their owners expected to be absent only briefly. The temple of the Aten was not, as is frequently stated, completely razed under Horemheb, who demolished the great temple which Akhenaten had built to the Disk at Karnak. The city of Akhetaten only gradually became anathema, shunned and feared by all; and Ramesses II did not hesitate to quarry from its sanctuary stones that pictured the heretic and his god, to use them as fill in the foundations and pylons of the temple he built to Amun at Hermopolis, a short distance across the river from the accursed site.

Tutankhamun might well have been forgotten by history, but as a result of the discovery of his Theban tomb, with its dazzling royal equipment all but intact, he is perhaps better known today than any other ancient ruler; his name seems likely, as he would have wished, to "live forever." He was a mere child when he came to the throne, only about eighteen when he died, and his reign was brief, lasting not more than ten years. It seems significant of the very gradual rise of resentment against the Amarna heresy and the family that promulgated it that Tutankhamun was permitted to ascend the throne at all. Even more, he ruled under the tutelage of Ay, the putative uncle of Akhenaten, who had been a pillar of the heretical faith, and it was the aged Ay who (as has previously been noted) briefly succeeded the boy king as ruler of the Two Lands.

Both Ay and his ward had recanted; they emphasized their orthodoxy in every pictured scene, every text of their reigns. On a stela which Tutankhamun erected at Karnak and which Horemheb later usurped, he records that he expelled deceit from the Two Lands and re-established Maat "as in its first time." He adds that he had found the temples desolate and overgrown with vegetation; "their halls were a footpath." The gods had fled and turned a deaf ear to the entreaties of suppliants. All this the young King changed. He rebuilt and refurbished the temples, replaced the vanished cult images with statues of "fine gold from the highlands," re-established the priesthood, carefully choosing men "from among the notables of their towns" for the divine service. He doubled, tripled, and quadrupled, so he claimed, the treasure of the temples, especially searching his heart for acts of devotion to Amun. In his piety and bounty he "went beyond what had been done since the time of the ancestors."

His apostasy was of no avail. Future generations sent Tutankhamun and his co-regent and successor, Ay, into limbo along with the heretic Akhenaten. The Eighteenth Dynasty ends with the name of Amunhotep III. There, too, ends the history of Thebes as a capital. Though it was nominally the seat of the first rulers of the Nineteenth Dynasty, their activities were centered chiefly in Lower Egypt, and it was in the Delta that Ramesses II, the third king of the dynasty, established his "fair throne, after the pattern of Thebes."

Akhenaten and his sole god were as if they had never been. But though Thebes became richer than ever before, The City and Egypt as a whole never recovered from the shock of the reformation. Thebes was no longer a world center, the capital of an Empire, and Egypt never fully regained her supremacy in the ancient world. The City flourished as a shrine. It was for centuries to come a place of pilgrimage, a place to be buried in. "One comes to port in Thebes," says a writer of the Nineteenth Dynasty. "The impious enter not into the Place of Truth. How fortunate he who lands there—he shall become a transfigured being!"

King Ay, who had awaited his chance so patiently, enjoyed the rule for a scant five years. He was succeeded by Horem-heb, who established what amounted to a military dictatorship. Horemheb had been a commander of the army under Akhenaten. He claimed, after his accession, to have "acted as vice-regent of the Two Lands over a period of many years," and there is reason to believe that he controlled the administration, at least in the North, during the reign of Akhenaten and his weak successors. Although Horemheb appears on ancient lists as the last king of the Eighteenth Dynasty, some modern historians would make him the first ruler of the Nineteenth Dynasty. In fact, however, since he was apparently related by blood or marriage neither to the pharaohs who preceded him nor to those who followed him, his rule might better be regarded as an interregnum. During some thirty years on the throne, he did much to bring order to a troubled land, ruthlessly endeavoring to erase all trace of the cult of the Aten and all memory of the kings under whom he had risen to power—Akhenaten, Smenkhkare, Tutankhamun, and Ay.

Horemheb was succeeded in about 1320 by a general whom he had made his vizier. Ramesses I, the founder of the Nineteenth Dynasty, was already an old man and ruled only briefly. Under the greatest of his successors, Seti I, Ramesses II, and Ramesses III, Egypt gained an ephemeral control over part of its former sphere of influence in Asia. Gold still poured into the country from Nubia. Constructions became larger and more massive; the most conspicuous of those now standing at Thebes are the work of the early Ramessides, for Amun was still the King of the Gods, and his Holy City waxed in splendor. But the country seethed in discontent. It was never again, save briefly, completely unified. Foreign enemies multiplied. Egypt was harassed from East and West, and new peoples pressed from beyond the Mediterranean.

The treasury was depleted by constant warfare. As the Nineteenth and Twentieth Dynasties wore on, the domestic administrative machinery began to stall. There were strikes by hungry workmen, spasmodic revolts, palace intrigues, tomb robberies on a grandiose scale—even the dead kings were stripped of their treasure. Religion relapsed almost entirely into superstition. A desperate populace turned to magic, and weak rulers of the ebbing New Kingdom resorted to oracles of Amun to uphold their law.

In the Twenty-first Dynasty, so-called priest-kings temporarily asserted the rule of the god over Thebes and to some extent over Egypt. Already under Ramesses XI, a general named Herihor had attained the post of High Priest at Thebes and arrogated to himself kingly power and royal titles, though the puppet Pharaoh still nominally held the throne. Herihor was not only high priest, but viceroy of Nubia and Southern vizier; and he shared the actual rule of Egypt with the vizier of the North, a man called Smendes, who ultimately became the founder of the Twenty-first Dynasty. That feeble dynasty ruled from Tanis. Its rulers sent their eldest sons to be the priest-kings of Thebes, but the divided rule proved ineffectual. Rival factions arose in Thebes, and even the divine oracle was insufficient to hold them in check. The Twenty-second Dynasty saw Egypt under the rule of Libyans, who had taken advantage of internal strife to establish themselves at Herakleopolis and who now, with the aid of the army, gained control of the Two Lands. They were followed by a dynasty of Ethiopians; and finally, after the short but brilliant revival of the seventh and sixth centuries under native pharaohs established at the Delta city of

Sais, the rule passed forever into foreign hands, to remain there until our own times.

Ramesses XI was the last of the kings to be buried at Thebes. Though later kings still offered their devotion to Amun, The City was never again a royal residence; and its wealth and influence gradually declined with the decaying civilization. A series of conquerors despoiled it of its treasure. Its temples gradually fell into ruin. When Caesar Augustus, the last of the rulers who added to the great sanctuary of Amun-Re, had himself pictured at Karnak as presenting a figure of Maat to Amun, Ptah, and Hathor, it was an alien order that he proffered, in a shabby, neglected temple, to impress with the might of Rome those Thebans who had vainly revolted against his tax collectors.

A few centuries later, Christian monks swarmed into the Thebaid. Anchorites dwelt in the tombs of onetime nobles. Within the sheltering precincts of temples, squatters erected hovels of mud brick. Ancient sanctuaries were converted into churches; the figures of pagan gods and divine kings were hacked out or covered over with plaster, on which were superimposed rude frescoes of the saints of Christendom.

The destruction of Thebes has continued down to the present. Its stones have been carried off for reuse in local construction; some of its despoiled tombs still shelter fellahin and their livestock; clandestine diggers still search for treasure, destroying more than they find. While ill-equipped archaeologists of the past contributed to the ruin by reckless digging, modern archaeologists have developed a conscience. They seek knowledge instead of loot, and many Egyptians, formerly indifferent, are beginning to appreciate and cherish the relics of their own great past. The emphasis now is on restoration and preservation.

But the awakening is too late by many centuries. Scholars of the present, who seek to clear and restore the ruins of Thebes, are able to conjure up only a shadowy evocation of The City as it once was. Only a meager part of the magnificence that Amunhotep III looked upon now survives, and that small part is sadly decayed. The color, the glitter, the sound of music, the fragrance of flowers and incense have vanished from the temples, along with the white-robed priests. The teeming festival crowds that hailed the majesty of gods and kings have been replaced by gaping school children and camera-happy tourists. Some of them snigger at the figures of the divinities who protected The City when it was the Scepter of Egypt.

Chronological Table

[After W. C. Hayes in *Cambridge Ancient History*, I, Chapter VI[1]]

(Only the reigns of the Eighteenth Dynasty are listed in full)

Prehistory: Before 3100 B.C.

Archaic Period (Dynasties I–II) : 3100–2686 B.C.

Old Kingdom (Dynasties III–VI) : 2686–2181 B.C.

First Intermediate Period (Dynasties VII–X) : c. 2181–2040 B.C.

Middle Kingdom (Dynasties XI–XII) : 2133–1786 B.C.

  Dynasty X (Herakleopolitan) and Dynasty XI (Theban) are partly contemporaneous

Second Intermediate Period (Dynasties XIII–XVII) : 1786–1567 B.C.

  Hyksos Period (Dynasty XV) : 1674–1567 B.C.

New Kingdom (Dynasties XVIII–XX) : 1567–1085 B.C.

  Eighteenth Dynasty: 1567–1320 B.C.

Ahmose	1570–1546 B.C.
Amunhotep I	1546–1526 B.C.
Thutmose I	1525–1512 B.C.
Thutmose II	1512–1504 B.C.

1 There is considerable variance among scholars on the dates of Egyptian history. I have followed in this book a table, here somewhat condensed, which was furnished to me by the late William Christopher Hayes, who prepared it in connection with his contribution on Egyptian chronology written for the revised *Cambridge Ancient History*, I, Chapter VI.

Hatshepsut	*1503–1482 B.C.
Thutmose III	*1504–1450 B.C.
Amunhotep II	1450–1425 B.C.
Thutmose IV	1425–1417 B.C.
Amunhotep III	1417–1379 B.C.
Amunhotep IV	1379–1362 B.C.
Smenkhkare	*1364–1361 B.C.
Tutankhamun	1361–1352 B.C.
Ay	1352–1348 B.C.
Horemheb	1348–1320 B.C.

*Coregencies

Nineteenth Dynasty: 1320–1200 B.C.

Ramesses I	1320–1318 B.C.
Seti I	1318–1304 B.C.
Ramesses II	1304–1237 B.C.

Twentieth Dynasty: 1200–1085 B.C.

Ramesses III	1198–1166 B.C.

Late Dynastic Period (Dynasties XXI–XXX): 1085–332 B.C.

Tanite Kings	1085–950 B.C.
Libyan Rule	950–730 B.C.
Kushite Rule	751–656 B.C.
Thebes sacked by Assyrians	663 B.C.
Saite Revival	663–525 B.C.
Persian Conquest	525–404; 341–332 B.C.

Conquest of Egypt by Alexander the Great: 332 B.C.

Bibliography

THE REFERENCES GIVEN HERE are, for the most part, confined to works written in the English language. Those marked with an asterisk contain comprehensive bibliographies.

Arkell, A. J. *A History of the Sudan to 1821.* 2d ed. London, 1961.

Baedeker, Karl. *Egypt and the Sudan.* Ed. by Georg Steindorff. 8th rev. ed. London and New York, 1929.

Breasted, James H. *Ancient Records of Egypt.* Chicago, 1906.

———. *A History of Egypt from the Earliest Times to the Persian Conquest.* 2d ed. London, 1927.

Brunton, Winifred M., *et al. Kings and Queens of Ancient Egypt.* London, 1925.

———. *Great Ones of Ancient Egypt.* London, 1929.

Bruyère, Bernard. *Deir el-Médineh. Le village* . . . . Fouilles de l'Institut français d'archéologie orientale du Caire, Tome XVI, 1939.

Černý, J. *Ancient Egyptian Religion.* London, 1952.

Edgerton, W. F. "The Government and the Governed in the Egyptian Empire," *Journal of Near Eastern Studies,* Vol. VI (1947), 152–60.

Egypt Exploration Society. *The City of Akhenaten.* (*Memoirs* 38, 40, 44.) London, 1923–51.

Erman, Adolf. *The Literature of the Ancient Egyptians.* Tr. by A. M. Blackman. London, 1927.

Faulkner, R. O. "Egyptian Military Organization," *Journal of Egyptian Archaeology,* Vol. XXXIX (1953), 32–47.

Frankfort, Henri. *Kingship and the Gods.* Chicago, 1948.

*Gardiner, Sir Alan. *Egypt of the Pharaohs.* Oxford, 1961.

*Hayes, William C. "Egypt: Internal Affairs from Tuthmosis I to the Death of Amenophis III," Pts. 1 and 2, *Cambridge Ancient History* (rev. ed.), II, chap. IX. Cambridge, 1962.

*———. *The Scepter of Egypt: A Background for the Study of Egyptian Antiquities in the Metropolitan Museum of Art.* 2 vols. New York, 1953, 1959.

Kees, Hermann. *Ancient Egypt: A Cultural Topography.* Ed. by T. G. H. James. Chicago, 1961.

Lefebvre, G. *Histoire des grands prêtres d'Amon de Karnak jusqu'à la XXIe Dynastie.* Paris, 1929.

Montet, Pierre. *Everyday Life in Egypt.* London, 1958.

Posener, Georges, *et al. Dictionary of Egyptian Civilization.* New York, 1962.

Säve-Söderbergh, T. "The Hyksos Rule in Egypt," *Journal of Egyptian Archaeology,* Vol. XXXVII (1951), 53–71.

———. *The Navy of the Eighteenth Egyptian Dynasty.* Uppsala, 1946.

Sauneron, S. *Les prêtres de l'ancienne Égypte.* Bourges, 1957. This book, rather inadequately translated, also appears in English under the title *The Priests of Ancient Egypt* (New York and London, 1960).

Smith, William Stevenson. *Ancient Egypt as Represented in the Museum of Fine Arts* [Boston]. 4th ed., rev. Boston, 1960.

*———. *The Art and Architecture of Ancient Egypt.* (Pelican History of Art.) Baltimore, 1958. Contains valuable references in the notes.

Steindorff, George, and Keith C. Seele. *When Egypt Ruled the East.* 2d ed., revised by Keith C. Seele. Chicago, 1957.

Wilson, John A. *The Culture of Ancient Egypt.* Chicago, 1959.

(Phoenix Books; originally published as *The Burden of Egypt* [1951].)

——. "Egyptian Texts," in J. B. Pritchard (ed.), *Ancient Near Eastern Texts Relating to the Old Testament*. Princeton, 1950.

Winlock, Herbert E. *Excavations at Deir el Bahri, 1911–1931*. New York, 1942.

——. *The Rise and Fall of the Middle Kingdom in Thebes*. New York, 1947.

Index

Index

Amunhotep IV: *see* Akhenaten
Anubis: 75, 142
Apepi (Hyksos ruler): 25
Apophis: 139
Army: *see* Military
Arzawa, princess of: in Amunhotep III's harem, 101
Aten: 190, 191, 192; temple of at Amarna, 58–59
Athribis: 157
Atum: 128, 129, 144
Atum-Re: 129, 132
Ay: 109, 186, 195, 196

Ba (concept of spirit): 145
Babylonia, princess of: in Amunhotep III's harem, 101–102
Bes: 67, 75
Book of the Dead: 144

Chariotry: *see* Military
Chariots: 23–24
Concubinage: 114–15
Conscription: *see* Military

Deir el Bahri: 17, 140
Deir el Medineh: 70, 73–76
Delta: early history, 14–15; subdued by Herakleopolitans, 16
Diodorus Siculus: 54, 116, 178; quoted, 14
Divorce: 116–17
Djeme: 136
Djer, King: 143
Dress: 68–69

Eastern (Arabian) Desert: 12
Education: of princes, 42–43; of scribes, 85–87
Egypt: cultivable land, 178, 180; population, 178–83; *see also* Lower Egypt *and* Upper Egypt
Eighteenth Dynasty: 196, 197
Ethiopian Dynasty: 198

Festivals: 158–59; New Year's Day, 160; sed festival (royal jubilee), 41, 160–61; Beautiful Feast of the Valley, 161, 162; Most Beautiful Feast of Opet, 161, 162–65

207

Index